Connecting With Your Asperger Partner

of related interest

The Asperger Couple's Workbook
Practical Advice and Activities for Couples and Counsellors
Maxine Aston
ISBN 978 1 84310 253 3

Love, Sex and Long-term Relationships
What People with Asperger Syndrome Really Really Want
Sarah Hendrickx
ISBN 978 1 84310 605 0

Alone Together
Making an Asperger Marriage Work
Katrin Bentley
ISBN 978 1 84310 537 4

22 Things a Woman Must Know
If She Loves a Man with Asperger's Syndrome
Rudy Simone
Foreword by Maxine Aston
ISBN 978 1 84905 803 2

Connecting With Your Asperger Partner

Negotiating the Maze of Intimacy

Louise Weston
Foreword by Tony Attwood

Jessica Kingsley *Publishers*
London and Philadelphia

First published in 2010
by Jessica Kingsley Publishers
116 Pentonville Road
London N1 9JB, UK
and
400 Market Street, Suite 400
Philadelphia, PA 19106, USA

www.jkp.com

Library of Congress Cataloging in Publication Data
A CIP catalog record for this book is available from the Library of Congress

British Library Cataloguing in Publication Data
A CIP catalogue record for this book is available from the British Library

ISBN 978 1 84905 130 9

Dearest Gay,

You're so amazing, tenacious and strong
A woman of substance and grace
Committed to husband, family and friends
'Never quit' is a phrase you embrace.

You've risen and taken the challenge
To reconnect with your Aspie mate
Regaining your own identity
Finding it wasn't too late.

You encouraged me to keep going
Persevering, long beyond the setting sun
You sat with me for hours on end
Laughing and laughing 'til the book was done.

You've helped me reach my goal
On you I can depend
I'm dedicating this book to you
Gay, you're a wonderful friend.

Contents

Acknowlegements

First, I give thanks to God for opening my eyes and saving our marriage. I'm forever thankful to my husband, Graham, because he stood by me through the difficult times. He also encouraged me to discover my identity and purpose. Graham's thoughts on how his brain works and how he views life have been inspirational in writing this book. The more I understand the Aspie world, the easier it is to relate to him. Graham and I now enjoy a happier relationship, with special connecting moments because we understand and accept our differences. I appreciate Graham's support during the past two-and-a-half years while I've been writing this book, especially his expert assistance with designing the figures, diagrams and charts.

Assistance from Helen, Rachel and others from Jessica Kingsley Publishers was essential in the completion of my manuscript. Professor Tony Attwood has been an inspiration to me; I am eternally grateful for his invaluable information given through books, seminars and DVDs. I highly recommend his book, *The Complete Guide to Asperger's Syndrome*.

Katrin Bentley's book *Alone Together* changed our marriage and is also highly recommended. I found the practical suggestions very helpful and insightful in understanding my husband's behaviour and meltdowns. I realized that in order to save our relationship, *I* had to change, as it was far more difficult for Graham to do so. It was Katrin who first encouraged me to write this book.

Ultimately, I couldn't have written this book without the dedication and commitment of five inspiring people: Marie Seltenrych, Gay Wallace, Tammy Copley, Jason Thompson and Isobel Hoole. Words can't express my gratitude to them for the endless hours of proof-reading, encouragement and constructive ideas that helped to make this book a reality.

I am extremely grateful for the assistance of professionals: Winnie Lau and Penny Threlfall. Also, the many proof-readers are to be thanked; amongst them are Carol Grigg, Maureen Treloar, Tracy Churchill, Carolyn Christopher and Darryl and Lindy Fraser. I appreciate Cheree Davis, Susan Gordon and Isobel Hoole; without their input *In the Zone Charts* wouldn't have been perfected. Special thanks to the members of support groups who have shared their perspectives.

Foreword

When someone falls in love with a partner whose personality and abilities include the characteristics of Asperger's Syndrome, the depth and quality of mutual love is intoxicating. The relationship is described by both partners in superlatives, each besotted by the other. When rating the quality of the relationship, the neurotypical partner may describe a sense of euphoria and optimism that is greater than usually occurs for a relationship between neurotypicals. However, over time, perhaps after living together for several years, there can be a realization that the quality of the relationship is not what was originally anticipated by both partners. The intense feelings of love, compassion, tolerance and mutual understanding are slowly eroded by experience. The neurotypical partner identifies characteristics of the Aspie partner that have become irritating or depressing. Emotions, experiences and responsibilities are not shared, needs and expectations are not fulfilled, communication breakdowns occur, conflicts arise over priorities, and increased anxiety leads to control issues. The neurotypical partner can experience a change in his or her sense of identity, with previously enjoyed experiences such as social occasions with friends becoming less frequent, and increasing feelings of loneliness within the relationship. The neurotypical partner gradually and reluctantly starts to 'mirror' the Aspie partner's behaviour, lifestyle and thinking in order to maintain the relationship.

The partner who has the characteristics of Asperger's Syndrome may also feel irritated and depressed. There may be a feeling of being unable to meet his or her partner's expectations in terms of social experiences, expression of inner thoughts and feelings, intimacy, coping with change, and household responsibilities from budgeting to taking care of the children. Stress can be considerable due to not understanding why there is criticism for contributing to a disappointing relationship, and why his or her natural behaviour should cause such distress and anguish. The partner with the characteristics of Asperger's Syndrome may not intuitively know what to do to rectify the relationship, and may feel guilt, shame and a sense of failure.

While all couples experience some of the above challenges and adjustments in maintaining a relationship, when one of the partners has the characteristics of Asperger's Syndrome the degree of these challenges and adjustments is greater, and the strategies to repair or enhance the relationship can seem elusive to both partners. Louise Weston has written *Connecting with Your Asperger Partner* as a relationship manual to enable both partners to understand each other's expectations and perspective, and provide advice on how to connect successfully from conversation to intimacy. The style is clear and engaging, the strategies realistic and practical and the overall theme positive and optimistic. I know that couples will have many 'eureka' moments in terms of explanations of thoughts and experiences, and that many relationships will be repaired and enhanced by incorporating her advice.

Tony Attwood
Minds and Hearts Clinic, Brisbane, Australia

About this book

To my reader: thank you for reading this book. It's my prayer that *Connecting with Your Asperger Partner* will contribute to healing in your relationship. As you read, it's important to complete the chapters in order, so that you'll understand how the concepts build on each other. This enables you to develop a strong basis for healing and reconnecting with your partner. We are all on different relationship journeys with our unique Aspies. Come with me and negotiate the maze of intimacy which leads to reconnecting, by learning about the four vital keys.

Positive change takes time, possibly taking more than a year to become evident. Achieving happiness in your relationship is attainable by implementing strategies suggested in this book. Stories of individuals have been included with their permission. Strategies and suggestions presented are derived from my personal opinions and experiences as an Aspie's wife and coordinator of a neurotypical (NT) support group. The information does not replace medical and psychological advice, but is intended to complement professional therapies.

Permission to photocopy

The following may be photocopied for personal or teaching purposes: Helpful Hints, The Steps to Self-discovery and Connecting, The Aspie's Energy Cup, The NT's Energy Cup, In the Zone: Green Zone is Where the Aspie is Relaxed, In the Zone: Orange Zone – Warning Signs of Impending Meltdown, In the Zone: Red Zone is Danger Zone (Don't Approach), Maslow's 'Hierarchy of Needs', The Aspie's World, The Aspie's Brain: A Central Processing Unit (Single Core) and The Ten Golden Keys to Connecting.

Characteristics of Asperger's Syndrome
Anxiety
Sensory overload problems
Practical, perfectionist, pedantic
Extreme frustration
Right, always right
Gifted
Emotionally drained
Rigid thinking, coupled with routine
Socially misunderstood

Special Interest
You need to understand their brain is wired differently
Need aloneness
Defensive
Relationship difficulties
Overly involved with details
Motor clumsiness; memory loss
Extreme intelligence

Strategies for the neurotypical
No expectations = no disappointments
Explain emotional and social cues
Understanding
Remain calm
One instruction at a time
Talk slowly and clearly
You must regain your identity; revitalize your life
Prepare your partner for upcoming events
Improve the relationship by backing off
Change yourself first; then the Aspie might change
Allow space
Love unconditionally!

Terms used

Aspie a term of endearment for a person with Asperger's Syndrome

AS Asperger's Syndrome

ASD Autistic Spectrum Disorder

NT (Neurotypical) 'a person who doesn't have an Autistic Spectrum or a neuro-developmental disorder, i.e. a person whose brain functions like the majority of people', as stated by Ashley Stanford on p.274 of her book, *Asperger Syndrome and Long-Term Relationships*

Special Interest 'having an intense interest in a particular subject, often associated with pleasure and the acquisition of knowledge about the physical rather than the social world' (which is how Tony Attwood explains it on p.141 of his book, *The Complete Guide to Asperger's Syndrome*)

Executive Secretary a supportive role where the NT can assist the Aspie with prioritizing and organizing tasks, as well as reminding them about appointments (again, see Attwood's book)

What is Asperger's Syndrome (AS)?

In *The Complete Guide to Asperger's Syndrome*, Professor Tony Attwood describes Asperger's Syndrome as a neurobiological condition where the brain is hardwired differently. Core features include: lack of social understanding, limited ability to have a reciprocal conversation, and an intense interest in a particular subject.

According to an Asperger Services Australia information card (published in 2007), some famous people like Mozart, Albert Einstein and Thomas Jefferson are believed to have experienced Asperger's Syndrome.

Helpful Hints

Looking after yourself

- Have adequate sleep and rest.
- Put your health needs first.
- Seek personal counselling.
- Be self-sufficient, not needy.
- Attend a partner's support group (ASD or NT).
- Rediscover your needs and goals.
- Be organized to reduce stress.
- Do something relaxing to rejuvenate your body.
- Enjoy support and time with friends and family.
- Maintain your 'energy cup'.
- Aim for 'quick recovery time'.
- Always have something to look forward to.

Relating to your partner

- 'Let go of expectations.'
- Seek professional help.
- Encourage your partner to enjoy their Special Interest or passion.
- Try to be as flexible as possible.
- Give *genuine* praise often.
- Don't retaliate.
- Never ridicule your partner.

Tips to improve communication

- Listen attentively.
- Give one request at a time.
- Allow extra time to respond to instructions and questions.
- Speak respectfully.
- Make no assumptions; say exactly what you mean (see *Solutions for Adults with Asperger Syndrome* by Juanita Lovett).
- Respond firmly, don't react.
- Be specific when you communicate.
- Use phrases such as, 'that's illogical' or 'that's not common sense'.
- Communicate by writing notes.
- Speak slowly and clearly.
- Give plenty of warning prior to social activities.
- Try to understand that your partner sees the world differently to you.

Chapter 1

Two Steps Forward, One Step Back

'Sometimes what seems like the darkest step we've ever been on comes just before the brightest light we've ever experienced.'(From p.33 of Just Enough Light for the Step I'm On *by Stormie Omartian)*

Let me assure you that you're not alone on this journey. The process of connecting begins with negotiating the maze of intimacy, while learning as much as you can about Asperger's Syndrome. Along the way you'll discover the importance of looking after yourself and regaining your identity, leading to reconnecting with your loved one. Sometimes, the relationship is moving ahead; other times, it's in reverse. A helpful saying to remember is, 'Two steps forward, one step back.'

This chapter introduces the *four vital keys*, which if implemented, may improve your well-being and the way you relate to your partner. The keys are: learn about AS, 'let go of expectations', maintain your 'energy cup' and aim for 'quick recovery time'. The Steps to Self-discovery and Connecting are also outlined (see p.24). At the moment, your situation may seem desperate. Hold on to hope and be patient a little longer. Begin to move forward one step at a time.

Don't give up on your partner

If you love your partner, isn't it best to love them as they are? Consider this: if they had Alzheimer's disease or diabetes instead of AS, would you love or treat them any differently? Ultimately, it's at this moment that your partner needs you more than ever. Living with AS can be difficult. You may think, 'It's tough and I don't know how long I can hang in there.' Throughout this book, you'll find numerous helpful strategies to assist you in dealing with AS and connecting with your partner.

Take one step at a time

It's likely that you've been through a lot already and you may be at the 'end of your tether'. That's probably why you're reading this book. Will you commit to just *one* year? Currently, one year may seem like a lifetime when actually it's a small part of your life. Practise the strategies in this book and you'll see an improvement in the way you relate to your partner. Can you:

- find yourself again?
- seek personal and marital counselling?
- learn as much as possible about AS?

The four vital keys

Key 1: Learn about AS

Useful resources include: books, seminars, the internet, educational DVDs and your doctor or psychologist. The knowledge gained will help you understand the frustration, anger and unusual behaviour of your partner. Subsequently, relating becomes easier as you comprehend how the Aspie's brain works. Joining the AS association in your area is another way to keep up-to-date with the latest research. This association may also recommend support groups, counsellors and other helpful agencies.

Key 2: 'Let go of expectations'

'Letting go' or 'having no expectations' of the Aspie is vital. If you have *no* expectations of your partner, they feel relieved of the burden to conform to your way of doing things (see Chapter 2). This allows you and your partner to feel more relaxed and free to work on regaining your *individual* identities (see Chapter 10).

Key 3: Maintain your 'energy cup'

Currently, it may take up to three days to recover from your Aspie's meltdowns. For this reason, it's vital that you look after yourself by making time to fulfil your spiritual, emotional, physical, intellectual and mental needs. This will boost your self-esteem and confidence, enabling you to cope more effectively when your partner is anxious or in 'meltdown mode'. Strategies for looking after yourself and filling your energy cup will be discussed in detail in Chapter 3.

Key 4: 'Quick recovery time'

Quick recovery begins with refusing to listen to harsh words, staying calm and learning techniques to communicate more effectively with your partner. The second step is to ensure you receive adequate sleep so that you can cope better with the Aspie's meltdowns. In short, always stay one step ahead of the Aspie. Walking away and not accepting verbal abuse is imperative. The sooner you do that the faster you'll recover and regain your energy.

It's important to speak in a *respectful* manner to your Aspie. Using the 'broken record technique' is one way of remaining in control (as Kotzman and Kotzman suggest in their book, *Listen to Me, Listen to You*). An anonymous NT married to an Aspie for 48 years suggests that if your partner is shouting at you or frustrated about something, try saying these phrases in a calm, firm voice:

- I'm not able to talk about this right now.
- I'll discuss it in the morning.
- We'll come back to this later when you're not so anxious.
- I can't talk to you when you're upset.
- I'll discuss it later.
- We'll talk about this after you've had a rest.
- I can't understand what you're saying right now. I'll be back later.

If the Aspie follows you or continues to berate you when you use these phrases, either walk away and say nothing, or say, 'I'm happy to talk with you when you're calmer'. It's important *not* to engage in fights and to try not to take blunt and harsh words personally (see Chapter 8). The earlier in the interaction that you walk away, the more likely frustration meltdowns will decrease.

One woman shared her story:

I'm learning to walk away if my husband starts to raise his voice. If I do that early enough in the conversation, he may come back to me five minutes later. He never apologizes properly but attempts to by saying, 'I thought you said...' I can see he is gaining insight into the dynamics of the situation by processing and analysing his thoughts and what was said by the other person. (Anon 2008)

Implement communication and coping strategies

Conventional communication techniques don't usually work with an Aspie because their brain is wired differently. AS/NT relationships are not the same as typical relationships. Subsequently, new ways of communicating need to be learnt. It takes far less time and energy to discover new ways of relating in comparison to the time currently spent fighting. Skills such as speaking literally, clearly and with intent will eventually bring some harmony to your relationship.

Experiment with new ways of relating

If what you're currently doing isn't working, try something new. A useful technique is to give one instruction at a time, instead of expecting your partner to multi-task. Aspies are so drained from the events of the day that added pressure to remember instructions increases their anxiety. Communication difficulties, combined with high stress levels, may culminate in unnecessary arguments. Subsequently, decreased self-esteem, depression and exhaustion in either partner can result in gradual breakdown and end of the relationship.

Coping with meltdowns

Throughout this book, you'll discover ways to deal with the Aspie's harsh words and methods to resolve conflict. *In the Zone Charts* are helpful tools which outline ways of predicting meltdowns (see Chapter 9). They also offer proven practical strategies to assist in calming your partner and decreasing the frequency and severity of meltdowns. *In the Zone Charts* consist of three colour-coded charts. 'Green zone' is when the Aspie is relaxed. 'Orange zone' is when they're becoming stressed and 'red zone' is when they've exploded.

Adopt appropriate healthy boundaries

You need boundaries to protect yourself from being hurt. Some Aspies prefer boundaries but may have difficulty knowing where they stand and what's expected of them. Therefore, it may help to clearly explain or write down the boundary. Be precise by working out clear-cut rules for both of you and the family as a whole. When your partner is aware of and properly understands the 'rules', they tend to be very reliable in following them.

Aspies may be ignorant of people's boundaries, while at other times, be the most dutiful boundary respecter of all. Having one's boundaries violated regularly is upsetting. This leads to much resentment, so it's important to address these violations at the first possible opportunity. Setting healthy boundaries means appreciating your loved one as an individual, while at the same time being firm about what constitutes acceptable behaviour.

Change takes time

Reading this book will equip you with many coping strategies. Personal growth will result as you conquer the tough obstacles in this relationship. As you work on yourself, ways of relating to your partner will improve. Subsequently, growth can occur in your relationship with your Aspie. You will eventually find the light at the end of the tunnel. You may even catch a glimpse of the original person with whom you fell in love.

Your progression to a happy, healthy AS/NT relationship

The steps outlined in The Steps to Self-discovery and Connecting explain the continuous, ongoing process of regaining your identity and connecting with your partner. It may be helpful to copy the chart on the following page and place it where you're able to read it regularly.

Empathize with the Aspie

The Aspie's world is totally different from the world that you know. Their belief might be that *you* come from another planet, whereas your point of view may be that *they* come from another planet. Things that are ordinary in *your* world may not be ordinary in *their* world. Consequently, the Aspie may become confused about what's expected of them, resulting in frustration. Aspies may have difficulty noticing subtle emotional and social cues, and comprehending when to give empathy.

Imagine for a moment that you're an Aspie:

People are confusing and rules change. You're experiencing *constant* anxiety, frustration and confusion, as well as physical symptoms such as exhaustion, chest/stomach pains, palpitations and sweaty palms. Other issues to contend with are change, sensory overload and communicating with others. To sum it up: life is a real struggle. (Anon 2009)

The Steps to Self-discovery and Connecting

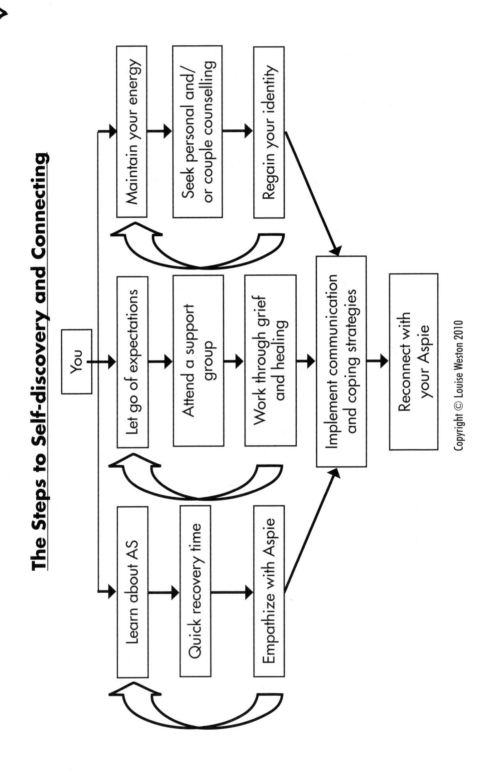

You

Learn about AS → Quick recovery time → Empathize with Aspie

Let go of expectations → Attend a support group → Work through grief and healing

Maintain your energy → Seek personal and/or couple counselling → Regain your identity

Implement communication and coping strategies → Reconnect with your Aspie

Copyright © Louise Weston 2010

You have just empathized with your partner. With time and knowledge, an understanding of their anxiety and frustration should become clearer, making it easier to put yourself 'in their shoes'.

Attend a support group

Strength and validation can be found through joining a partner's support group. Encouragement is gained through hearing successful stories and strategies that have worked for others. One new member stated, 'Understanding Aspergers has set me free like you would never believe' (Anon 2009).

Another new member shared:

> When I first came across the name 'Aspergers' and its associated characteristics, it was initially like a light had gone on behind a blackened, closed door. I was afraid to believe there could be a solution, when all I could feel was a shroud of darkness; not understanding what had happened to me – to us, a complete sense of failure and loss of who I was. The sense of aloneness was absolute. Then, as I read and discovered about AS, the door began to open and I could begin to trust it wasn't a false hope. The light shone and I knew I wasn't alone. Others understood. They too, had gone through a reflection of my life and I wasn't going mad! For me, the connection with others experiencing the same thing was the key to the first baby steps towards understanding and recovery. (Anon 2009)

Work through grief and healing

Grief is a natural reaction when you realize the relationship is a far cry from what you thought it would be. The five stages of the Grief Process and the 'Eight-Stage Healing Process' will be discussed in Chapter 10. Allow time to grieve the loss of the 'happily-ever-after' dream. With knowledge of AS, feelings of guilt for past behaviour may emerge. Try not to let these feelings take over. Remember, prior to awareness of AS, you made decisions based on your knowledge at the time. Don't allow guilt to rob you of happiness. Instead, remind yourself that you're on a *new* journey of learning and it's important to move forward to succeed.

Seek personal and/or couple counselling

Personal and marital counselling with a professional who has full understanding of AS can be extremely beneficial.

Regain your identity

Have you lost your sense of purpose and meaning in life? Start thinking about how you can regain it. Consult Chapter 10 for ideas. Finding yourself will give you strength to cope, no matter what lies ahead. As healing begins, connecting with your partner becomes easier. Embrace your new-found freedom and hope for a better future.

Reconnect with your partner

Consult Chapter 11 when you've started regaining your energy and identity to find helpful tips regarding how to reconnect with your partner.

Conclusion

Don't quit. Be patient and positive. Currently, it seems like nothing makes sense, your mind is foggy and overwhelmed, resembling many pieces of a jigsaw puzzle scattered everywhere. By the end of this book, the jigsaw will start to fit together and the picture will eventually become clear. Change takes time.

A light shines at the end of the tunnel, even though you may not see any light at the moment. Take the focus off striving to save your relationship and start rediscovering yourself. Remember, this is a process of 'Two steps forward, one step back'. Remind yourself regularly of the four vital keys to improving your relationship: learn about AS, 'let go of expectations', maintain your 'energy cup' and aim for 'quick recovery time'.

Chapter 2

'Letting Go of Expectations'

'I am not in this world to live up to your expectations and
you are not in this world to live up to mine.' (Fritz Perls, in
Dolliver's article 'Reflections on Fritz Perls's Gestalt Prayer')

Is it possible that you have too many expectations of your partner? Do you expect them to meet *all* your needs? It's unrealistic to think that another person can do this for you. You'll find that no relationship is perfect. Couples in any relationship find it difficult to meet all the needs of their partner.

This chapter discusses the importance of 'letting go of expectations' and also highlights the potential benefits of this to your emotional well-being. Two sayings that will be used interchangeably are: 'letting go of expectations' and 'no expectations = no disappointments'. Although this chapter asks you to adjust or 'let go of' your expectations, it's still perfectly reasonable for you to retain *some* expectations.

What are the *minimum* realistic expectations of partners in an AS/NT relationship? Some reasonable expectations are to spend at least a few hours a week together, communicating or interacting, even if it's just watching a favourite TV show. It's quite realistic for a partner to have certain expectations of their loved one such as to respect, love, protect and so on, but remember, no one can ever fully meet all the needs of another person.

What are expectations?

Expectations are preconceived ideas – something that we demand, hope for, or assume that our partner will do for us. Your partner may feel obligated or pressured to meet your needs, which adds to their anxiety and frustration. The fact remains that no one is obligated to another person.

If you do have expectations, this can further complicate the issues that the Aspie must contend with and adds unnecessary pressure to the relationship. If you go into a situation expecting nothing, you have a decreased chance of becoming anxious and stressed. It follows that if you're calm, it's more likely that the Aspie will be too.

Listen to an NT wife's advice:

> It's better to go into a situation with no expectations and be pleasantly surprised, than to have even some expectations (realistic or not) and be constantly disappointed. The Aspie can pick up the NT's tension and anxiety when they're asking something of the Aspie. They in turn become tense, anxious and are far more likely to escalate to a meltdown, than to complete the request. It's better to talk about important matters such as the house or yard maintenance, parenting issues and finances, when the Aspie is relaxed. Decide on what needs to be done away from the time of action. Aspies dislike being controlled and respond better to suggestions and delegation. If compliance is an issue, boundaries need to be negotiated. Counselling may be helpful in this area. (Anon 2009)

Expectations are different from responsibilities

A responsibility is something that someone is accountable for. Examples include going to work, paying the bills and looking after the children. Your Aspie partner might forget to pay the bills or collect the children from school, so they may need to be reminded or encouraged at the appropriate time.

Should you have any expectations?

It's reasonable to have some expectations but don't expect others to continually meet your needs or keep their promises. This pertains to family, friends, children, employers and work colleagues. For example, if you're looking forward to meeting a friend for coffee and they ring to cancel at the last moment, why waste energy and time being annoyed? Maybe this wasn't the perfect time to meet? Now you have a few precious moments to yourself. Make the most of them. In the *Bible*, in Ecclesiastes 3:1, it says, 'There is a time for everything, and a season for every activity under heaven'.

Expectations can be very high

Your expectations of the Aspie can be very high, especially if you're desperate to have your emotional needs fulfilled. Do you have the courage to let go of fixed ideas of how your partner should relate?

Aspies don't like us to have expectations of them as they may interpret this as controlling. Perhaps this saying may help: 'If you don't have any expectations, you won't have any disappointments'. Many partners have found this to be a useful quote to help them deal with the daily issues in an AS/NT relationship.

Letting go of expectations is the most important key in improving the relationship with your Aspie. At first, this is a *really difficult concept* to understand and some people have taken a year or more to comprehend it fully.

What does 'letting go of expectations' mean?

If you have unrealistic expectations of your partner, perhaps it's time to let these go. Relinquishing preconceived thoughts and demands releases your partner from the burden of fulfilling expectations that they may not be able to meet. You'll be surprised how freeing this is for both of you.

What does 'no expectations = no disappointments' mean?

At first, when you hear this saying, it seems like a totally foreign concept. However, when you start using it on a daily basis, it can become second nature. It will also be very beneficial in other areas of your life, not just in the relationship with your Aspie.

If you don't have any expectations of the Aspie, they will be less confused and more relaxed because the pressure of having to meet your needs is removed. Listed below are examples of what letting go of expectations means. Try to understand that your Aspie might not be able to:

- be romantic
- know when to give you a hug
- automatically meet your emotional needs (this doesn't come naturally to them)
- remember to do what you've asked them to do
- be understanding
- know how to woo you

- complete chores

- know what would be an appropriate gift for you

- understand what to do in a social situation.

Try not to:

- expect empathy/caring

- expect flowers (or whatever you hope for)

- expect dinner to be cooked the way you requested. If you were looking forward to chicken, and beef was cooked, does it really matter? Be grateful that the dinner was cooked for you at all

- rant and rave every time the Aspie forgets to do something. Often, they can't help it.

Successful stories that demonstrate letting go of expectations
Story 1

Driving home from a week's holiday on my own, I prepared myself for the AS/NT world. Deep down, I was hoping that he would come through the door, saying, 'I missed you so much,' accompanied by a big kiss and cuddle. When this didn't happen, I wasn't upset because I had reminded myself, 'Don't forget, no expectations = no disappointments.' (I remind myself of this a few times each day.)

The minute my partner came home, I noticed how stressed he was. He looked exhausted and had a stress rash all over his face. The first thing he said was, 'I've had a terrible week.' Once again, it was 'all about him.' I don't mind that, as I love him. However, it's important that I ensure my needs are communicated. I listened to him talk for a while and then excused myself.

Excited about my news, I rang a friend for a chat and I also wrote in my journal. These two things helped me to feel better. Later, my Aspie approached me to find out how my holiday was. By allowing him space to deal with his frustrations, I was rewarded because he was genuinely interested in my news about the holiday. (Anon 2008)

Tip: Protecting your own interests by ensuring that your needs are met elsewhere in a healthy way is important. It's not that the Aspie doesn't care about what you have to say. They might just have too many thoughts to process at that particular time, so be unable to focus on *your* needs.

Story 2

Even when your Aspie has spent a considerable amount of time on their Special Interest, don't make the mistake of presuming they will be cooperative and helpful with household jobs. The more you pressure them, the more likely they will resist doing what you've asked.

If you've discussed, as a couple, what jobs need to be done, ensure a list of these jobs is written down. This list could include who is responsible for which job, low or high priority jobs and a time-frame for completion. A time-frame is important because then the Aspie can complete the task in their own time and not feel you're controlling them. It's more likely they will follow through on completing the jobs if they're delegated because the Aspie feels empowered by contributing to the household. If this doesn't work, 'Plan B' could be to hire outside help to do the jobs. If you take this path, your partner might realize how much the completion of these jobs means to you and the family. Hopefully, they will respond better next time. (Anon 2008)

Story 3

My Aspie was away all week on a fishing trip with his friends. He had a wonderful time relaxing and enjoying himself immensely. A couple of days after he had returned home and settled back into the routine, I asked him to mow the lawn, as it had become quite long with recent rain. I had to go out on business, so it had been agreed that he would do the lawn while I was out, because he was playing golf the next day.

As I was driving home, I reminded myself 'no expectations = no disappointments'. Secretly, I hoped that he had turned over 'a new leaf'. As I drove into the yard, I couldn't help but notice that the mowing wasn't done. Instead of becoming incredibly upset, angry and tense, while saying 'no expectations = no disappointments', I went into the house and found him asleep.

In the past, I would have exploded. I greeted him and waited for him to respond. He sheepishly said, 'I haven't done the mowing,' to which I replied, 'It really does need doing, love.' He got off the bed and said, 'I'm going to do the mowing now. I waited until it was cool.' I replied, 'Oh that would be great. It always looks wonderful when you mow.' Later that evening, he surprised me by taking me out to dinner and a movie. (Anon 2009)

Your Aspie may not be able to meet your needs

Due to their structural and functional brain differences (discussed in Chapter 14), the Aspie may be unable to comply with your standards of how a partner should behave. This can lead to many misunderstandings and arguments.

If the 'no expectations' or 'letting go of expectations' rule is followed, these arguments can be avoided, as one partner doesn't feel obligated to do something to make the other happy. It's unfair to presume that another person is responsible for your happiness. Emotions are feelings that can be controlled. Happiness is a choice, as much as anger, sadness and so on. Despite how your Aspie treats you, it's *your choice* how you respond to situations.

Avoid anticipating

Do you tend to predict what your partner will or won't do? If you let go of these expectations, communication will improve. If you don't anticipate what will happen, both your stress levels and those of the Aspie will decrease. Encourage your partner to be spontaneous, rather than tense. If things are allowed to happen naturally, this may result in some unexpected, pleasant surprises. Make the most of the spontaneous moments.

Let go of preconceived ideas

Over time, preconceived ideas of how your partner should respond to certain situations have developed. Let go of these ideas, become flexible and give yourself permission to be free and happy, thereby decreasing the stress in the household. When you give your loved one the gift of choosing what's right for them, it strengthens your ability to choose what's right for you. Most people prefer not to be told how to think, feel or behave, especially Aspies. Sometimes, NTs can expect too much from their partners. Is it any wonder that difficulties are experienced in AS/NT relationships! In her book *Codependent No More*, Melody Beattie describes this:

> Most of us have expectations...about how we want people to behave. But it is better to relinquish expectations, so we can detach. It is better to refrain from forcing our expectations on others or refrain from trying to control the outcome of events, since doing so causes problems and is usually impossible anyway. (p.208)

One NT wife's view:

> I firmly believe that you can have *no* expectations, rather than negative expectations. It means coming into a situation on neutral grounds, rather than preparing yourself for the worst. You assess the situation and then respond accordingly. If you do this, you're far less likely to be disappointed because you don't have unrealistic expectations. (Anon 2008)

Try to change your mind-set

Certain expectations and beliefs are instilled into our brains before we even reach adulthood. Through parents, education, culture, 'societal norms', religion and media, we're taught to have expectations of others. Some romantic comedies or novels portray stereotypes of how mothers, fathers, lovers and heroes should be.

It's common for girls from around the age of six to daydream of their wedding day. They dream of the beautiful dress they will wear in many years to come. Before they even have a boyfriend, they may have the whole wedding day planned in their mind. Also, they conjure up what the perfect groom will look like and how they will play 'happy families' when they're married. We all know that one day this fantasy will come crashing down. Are you living in a fairytale world where you have high expectations of how your partner will meet all your needs and be *responsible* for your happiness?

Are you willing to take the risk?

If you adopt the 'no expectations' or 'letting go' rule, there might be an element of concern that your needs won't be met by the Aspie. Currently, it's quite likely that your needs aren't being met anyway. It's possible that your Aspie will repeatedly *not* be able to meet your expectations, especially if they have trouble realizing what your needs are. This could result in disappointment, which means you'll be dissatisfied and an endless cycle of confusing misunderstandings and arguments may follow.

By taking a risk and trying this strategy, there *can* be improvement in your relationship. If you stop having expectations of your partner, their performance anxiety will be reduced, possibly resulting in them drawing a little closer and you receiving some unexpected attention. This may take time, sometimes a long time. Eventually, you'll experience increased freedom and decreased conflict. Consequently, the Aspie is able to work on their identity, while you work on yours. What do you have to lose by taking the risk?

Detach emotionally from your partner

Ask yourself honestly, 'What do I need to do to *move on* with my life? Am I exhausted?' If warmth and spontaneity are missing or limited in your relationship, you may long for affection and attention from your partner. Instead of being enmeshed and clingy, work on becoming emotionally independent. It's necessary to distance yourself emotionally from your partner to avoid being constantly hurt. In order to protect your vulnerability, try and discover the emotional distance that best suits your relationship.

If you're too dependant on your partner, how do you detach emotionally? The following suggestions have been kindly offered anonymously by a woman married to an Aspie for 48 years:

- Become more self-sufficient.

- Build your own life.

- Avoid relying on the Aspie for anything.

- Let the Aspie do whatever they can, for example, if they're good at cooking, encourage this.

- Don't wait around for them to do what you expect. Sometimes, doing the task yourself quietly and without fuss is easier.

Tip: Emotionally detach from your partner with love, in a bid to work on yourself.

What are the benefits of letting go of expectations?

- Reduces disappointment.

- Gives you freedom because you're not carrying around potential anger and disappointment.

- Conserves energy.

- Provides *more time* for you to do the things you enjoy, rather than constantly waiting for your partner to meet your needs.

- Reduces anxiety and tension, thereby decreasing the frequency of meltdowns.

- May draw your partner closer to you, especially if they feel emotionally safe.

Adopt appropriate healthy boundaries

Most people tend to blame others for their troubles. What other people do, including your partner, is no one else's business unless they're being abusive towards you or your family. A counsellor experienced in AS may be helpful in assisting you to establish mutually healthy boundaries. Having appropriate healthy boundaries means:

- not letting your partner control you and not controlling your partner. Neither of you are 'puppets on a string'

- being definite with your responses: make sure your 'yes' means 'yes' and your 'no' means 'no'

- not accepting abuse. Remember, abuse comes in many forms. Verbal and emotional abuse can be just as painful as physical abuse. If this occurs, you don't have to tolerate it. Inform your partner that it's unacceptable behaviour. If necessary, contact the authorities

- respecting your partner as they are, not the person you want them to be

- realizing that people are fallible and it's all right if they don't meet your psychological needs

- not judging your partner and placing conditions on the relationship. Instead, love unconditionally.

How to manage disappointment

Disappointments may occur more frequently in an AS/NT relationship. If unrealistic expectations are put on either partner, it's only natural that one partner will feel disappointed if expectations are not met.

You're not a failure for reverting to an old habit

Obviously, if you've been expecting a lot from your Aspie for several years, it will take some time for them to trust that you're changing. While learning new behaviour, it's quite possible to accidentally revert back to old ways. If this happens, don't dwell on it. You're not a failure for reverting to an old habit; it's just a reminder that you forgot to implement new ways of relating. As the saying goes, 'old habits die hard'. Acknowledge that you made a mistake. Apologize if needed and remind yourself of the 'no expectations' rule.

Remember, the process of letting go of expectations may take a year or more to comprehend fully and use naturally every day. Replacing old habits with new ones is easier than trying to change old habits.

Plan B

A good tip is always to have a Plan B in mind so that if the first plan fails and you're feeling disappointed, you can recuperate by participating in an alternative activity. This motivates you to keep going, especially if your Aspie has a meltdown or they need unexpected, solitary time.

Stick to the facts and keep the emotion out of it

Let your partner know that you're disappointed and why. Tell them that you're trying to understand their point of view. Provide facts, try not to be emotional, and don't go on and on. To an Aspie, this can be seen as whinging, punitive and controlling. It's likely that they 'caught on' the first time.

A positive is that if you don't ramble on about how disappointed you are, it's more likely the Aspie may make it up to you in their special, quirky way. Compared to you, they need longer to process what's happened, possibly requiring space to cope with the fact that they've disappointed you.

Take away tips

- Remember the benefits of having no expectations.
- Ensure that your unmet, emotional needs are fulfilled in other ways by calling a caring, empathic friend.
- Avoid anticipating.
- Let go of fixed ideas.
- Remember, the Aspie may not know automatically how to meet your emotional needs.
- Try to change your mind-set about having expectations.
- Adopt appropriate healthy boundaries.
- Aspies still have responsibilities. Expectations are different from responsibilities.

Conclusion

If you don't try this freeing technique, you'll never know if it truly works. Carol Grigg from Asperger Syndrome Partner Information Australia (ASPIA) stated in 2009:

> Having 'no expectations' or 'letting go of expectations' helps us emotionally to deal with the disappointment and frustration, removes a lot of sources and points of conflict, and generally helps us to cope better. I guess ideally we should change our expectations, but I think you have to do this from a place of having none. It's like dismantling the relationship and then working out how and what to re-build, and adopting realistic expectations. It all depends on the person with AS too, on just how able they are. (Personal communication)

Letting go of expectations is the most important key to improving the relationship with your Aspie. Implementation of this concept can decrease the amount of meltdowns, which in turn can give you and your family more opportunities for positive experiences. The benefits to your physical and emotional health and well-being are: increased energy, reduced anxiety and less tension for you and your family. Eventually, you'll have more time and freedom to enjoy uplifting activities.

Often, your partner may draw closer to you when 'no expectations' is implemented. The most wonderful moment of all is when you have *no* expectations and all of a sudden your Aspie surprises you with a genuine act of kindness or a cute, personal, quirky gesture. Examples include an impromptu hug, a bunch of flowers or a cooked meal. The finest gift that you can give your partner is to allow them to be relaxed and free to be themselves.

Remind yourself daily that you can only do your best and that you're responsible only for *your* attitude and *your* life. Having no expectations or letting go of expectations is a concept that allows you to move on with your own life and enhance your personal growth. Go ahead, follow your dreams and goals – move on and fulfil your potential. In order to do this, it's imperative to look after yourself and maintain your energy. This significant topic will be discussed in the next chapter.

Chapter 3

Maintaining Your 'Energy Cup'

*'We need to find a balance between letting go of our
expectations and remembering we are important, valuable
people who deserve to lead decent lives.' (From p.229
of the book* Codepedent No More *by Beattie)*

Are you becoming depleted of emotional and physical energy? Maintaining this energy is imperative because if *you're* emotionally strong, the effects of the Aspie's behaviour won't be as traumatic. Try always to stay one step ahead of your partner, so that you're strong enough to relate to them and respond calmly. When you look after your own needs, self-esteem and confidence will increase. Looking after yourself *first* will give you the energy necessary to care for your partner and family. This chapter describes tips and self-care suggestions to boost and maintain emotional and physical energy.

Look after your physical and mental health

If you're going through extremely difficult times resulting in a feeling of sheer exhaustion, it might be time to seek help from a support group, counsellor and/or your doctor. A lack of energy and a feeling of sadness could result in 'not wanting to get out of bed', or do the things that once gave you pleasure. Is there a possibility that you're depressed? Now is the time when you need support from others the most – whether it's emotional or practical assistance. Antidepressants and/or counselling have helped some partners to feel normal again, resulting in more effective coping skills surrounding their Aspie's behaviours. When you're starting to feel better, be wise how you use up your energy. Do you feel exhausted as a result of dealing with your partner and family? Keep reading to learn ways of increasing and retaining your energy. Remember to ensure that a reserve of energy is kept for unexpected illness and emergencies.

Adopt appropriate healthy boundaries

It's vital that you have good boundaries. If you need to do something for yourself to keep sane – *do it*. If you're exhausted and someone asks you to do something, it's all right to say 'no'. If you're conditioned constantly to do things for others, you may often feel guilty if you do actually say 'no'. Be strong!

Don't be concerned if the Aspie complains and tells you that you shouldn't be wasting time on yourself. They will often find fault with anything that takes your attention away from them.

The small amount of precious time you dedicate to yourself will be worth the effort. Aspies spend hours enjoying *their* Special Interest, so it's fair that *you* take the time needed to improve your health and well-being. One NT wife shared how a lack of boundaries affected her energy levels:

> I exhaust myself, trying to get my Aspie's attention. I constantly show affection and do nice things for him, which go unnoticed. The more I give, the more tired I become. Sadly, more often than not, I become angry because I don't receive any attention from my partner, leaving me feeling emotionally empty. I have the habit of turning it around and then I feel guilty, because I have wants and needs that aren't met.
>
> Recently, I realized that I have a lack of boundaries and unrealistic expectations. My partner doesn't see the things that I do for him. He will never understand how I feel because he doesn't comprehend what the problem is. Maintaining my energy and taking time out for me has been the key to my survival.
>
> I highly recommend a great book called *Boundaries* written by Cloud and Townsend. Their methods can be used in any situation, not just AS/NT relationships. It has a Christian slant to it, but personally I found this book very enlightening. (Anon 2009)

Lack of boundaries can lead to exhaustion

If boundaries are not established and maintained, the NT can become exhausted. Affective Deprivation Disorder (AfDD) can result (see Maxine Aston's website www.maxineaston.co.uk. She also discusses this disorder in *The Asperger Couple's Workbook*). AfDD can develop because the NT has unmet emotional needs, resulting in feelings of loneliness and affection deprivation. When a couple are oblivious to AS in their relationship, the Aspie can often be misunderstood, leading to unnecessary conflicts. However, an AS/NT relationship can blossom when both partners work together to understand and support each other. Simons and Thompson, on p.4 of their unpublished paper *Affective Deprivation Disorder*, stated:

> Affective Deprivation Disorder results from a relationship in which emotional needs are chronically unmet creating a sense of emotional deprivation. This in no way should be taken to mean that either partner is actively or deliberately depriving the other. The deprivation is created by the fact that the partners are emotionally out of sync and it is overly simplistic to say that one partner causes the deprivation of the other. Instead, the reality is that each partner may contribute to the dysfunction in different degrees. While the relational difficulties may have originated from one partner's emotional constraints, the other partner's reaction may exacerbate the tension leading to defensiveness and creating a spiralling effect.

To prevent AfDD, it's imperative that each partner communicates their needs to the other, as well as working on filling their individual energy cups.

Energy cup

It's really important to keep your energy cup as full as possible. Some NTs fill their cups by spending time with family and friends, while others feel refreshed by enjoying some time alone. NTs gain and retain energy a lot faster than Aspies. The Aspie's Energy Cup (p.42) and The NT's Energy Cup (p.43) explain the different ways Aspies and NTs fill their energy cups.

An NT's story:

> Before marriage, my partner and I discussed self-help books that had changed our lives. These books often described how others could emotionally drain us. During our courtship, my Aspie would frequently say he was emotionally drained. As a result, he wouldn't come to visit me for a day or so. The reason he gave was that he had to 'fill his energy cup',

meaning he needed a rest and some 'me time'. Here is an example of how my partner relates to the concept of the energy cup:

After my Aspie and I arrived home from a week's holiday in Tasmania, he stated that he felt completely drained from the holiday and had no reserves left. I presume he hated Tasmania because it was unfamiliar and the road rules kept changing. Also, holidays can be unpredictable and unstructured. He said, 'Don't have *any* expectations of me this week.'

My eyes were opened; I finally understood how a change in the routine can affect the Aspie. Since his diagnosis, *I've* changed and try to have no expectations of him. I know it's up to me to find my own happiness and contentment. I must fill my own energy cup. (Anon 2008)

Tip: The secret is to keep your energy cup at least three-quarters full. If you can do this, it's more likely that you'll be happy and better able to deal with your partner. So, how full is *your* energy cup?

Why do you need to look after yourself?

Do you sacrifice your needs and push yourself to keep supporting your Aspie? It's likely that you've always been the peacemaker and interpreter for your partner and family. This can be time consuming and draining to the point of physical and emotional exhaustion, often leading to illness. If you don't do something just for *you*, the consequence may be burnout. The prevention of burnout is vital in this busy, fast-paced life.

Make time for yourself

Don't feel guilty for taking time out for yourself. Practise this every day. Stop giving more than you're able to give. It won't be easy at first, but try to do something special for yourself on a daily basis.

The Aspie's Energy Cup

Increases energy through
Special Interests
and solitude

1/4 full of energy

1/2 full of energy

This 1/2 cup leaves just enough energy to survive normal daily stress. Therefore, when it comes to the relationship with the NT the Aspie has nothing left to give

An empty cup: no
energy left to give
to the NT partner

The Aspie may feel inadequate, as well as exhausted, because the NT demands time and attention from them. They are unable to give to the NT, resulting in frequent misunderstandings.

The NT's Energy Cup

Increases energy through relaxing activities like reading, walking, nature, sport, socializing and solitude

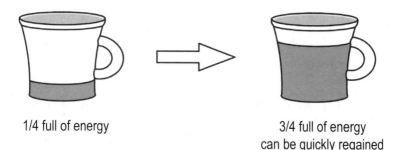

1/4 full of energy

3/4 full of energy
can be quickly regained

Social and emotional interpreter and peacemaker

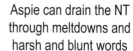

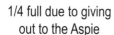

1/4 full due to giving
out to the Aspie

Aspie can drain the NT
through meltdowns and
harsh and blunt words

The NT lives in an affection desert – asks for more time and attention from the Aspie, resulting in frequent misunderstandings. The NT may not realize that the Aspie can't give anything to them. Consequently, both have nothing to give. This is the reason for the endless cycle of exhaustion. The solution is each individual must be responsible for filling their own cup. The optimal situation is if each person has their own cup that is at least three-quarters full at all times.

What drains your energy?

A busy schedule

Are you too busy to look after yourself? If so, what tasks can be delayed for another time? Deal with all the must-do important things first; go to work, look after your family and pay the bills. Learn to delegate to others and try to let the little things go.

Stress

An effective stress reducer that shows healthy respect for self and others is 'swapping hats':

> When I come home after work, shopping etc., I say to my husband, 'Love, I just need five minutes to catch my breath, change my clothes and go to the bathroom.' This space allows me to calm down, refocus and 'swap hats'. I'm then much better able to deal with whatever awaits me. (Anon 2010)

It can very stressful when changing from one task or role to another. Take a few minutes to recover from the task at hand by taking a breath, calming down and relaxing before 'putting on a new hat' and commencing the next task. This allows you to become calm, think more clearly and concentrate on problem solving, so that you can deal with stress while retaining your energy. It's really amazing the difference just a few stolen minutes can make.

Anger

People can be draining, especially when they're angry with you. How do you *feel* when someone yells at you?

An NT wife shared her story:

> One day, while travelling in another state, my partner and I went to a club for afternoon tea. I said to him, 'I'm going to the toilet and then I'm going to have a cup of tea and write my poem.' After I went to the toilet I forgot to wait for my husband. Totally exhausted from the meltdowns, I went and bought a cup of tea. As I was enjoying my tea, I thought I'd better ring him on his mobile to see where he was. I left a message explaining exactly where I was seated. Soon after, he bounded into the bistro, looking angry. As he sat down he spoke with an accusatory tone, saying, 'I didn't know where you were. Why didn't you wait for me outside the toilet? *I* wait for

you outside the toilet. *You* should wait for me outside the toilet. That's the rule everywhere we go.'

My Aspie was very upset and annoyed because I failed to stick to the 'rule'. Embarrassed by his outburst, I felt totally drained of energy. Casting my thoughts back to *Alone Together* [the book by Bentley], I remembered the 'energy theory'. Instead of retaliating, I apologized and firmly said, 'I'm very sorry that you couldn't find me. Is it okay now if I have my cup of tea and write my poem?' He said politely, 'By all means, have your cup of tea.'

I noticed that a simple apology and the distraction of my poem calmed him down. His facial expressions were now relaxed, instead of tense and grimaced. A few days later, I said to him, 'You know the other day, when you couldn't find me in the bistro, your face showed signs of stress. What made you suddenly relax?' He said, 'Well, the solution had happened, the conflict was over. There was no need to go on about it any more.'

From this statement, I realized that he doesn't like to go on and on about an issue. He would rather it be over quickly. According to him, everything is black or white. Further discussion is not required if the solution has been found. (Anon 2007)

Are you giving too much?

Take a clear look at your life. Apart from your Aspie, are there people who lean on you for excessive support? If you allow them to rely on you for too long, you'll become exhausted. Recognize your limitations. It's okay to say no. You need to distance yourself from people who drain you of energy.

Tip: Avoid giving too much or you may end up an emotional and physical wreck. It's okay and necessary to look after yourself.

Nurture yourself

Recognize and nurture the valuable person that you are. At times, your partner may not be in a position to express how much they value you, but deep down, most Aspies appreciate their NT partner. It's *vital* to nurture yourself. Once again, have no expectations. What are you currently doing to take care of yourself in the following areas: spiritual, emotional, physical, intellectual and mental?

Spiritual

We are all spiritual beings and at some point in our lives, most people seek to know if God is real or not. If you have a strong belief in God, it's likely you have an unshakable foundation of faith, beliefs and core values to carry you through any difficult situation. If you don't, it's helpful to believe in something. What is the basic belief system that gives you faith in your ability to keep pressing on during the hard times? What belief system reinforces your value as an individual?

Emotional

- Improve your self-esteem and confidence.

- Enjoy a favourite hobby or find a new one. Explore or develop your creative side by completing a short course, such as an art or cooking class.

- Spend time alone (without your partner) or with uplifting family and friends.

- Enjoy relaxation time. You deserve it! Give yourself permission to enjoy it, without feeling guilty. It's vital that *you* decide how to spend your relaxation time. Don't allow your partner to control or disturb it. When was the last time you pampered yourself? Some suggestions:

  - massage, facial or manicure
  - favourite activities: walking the dog, reading a good book
  - coffee and movie with a friend.

- Schedule fun times. Most people say that they feel exhilarated, happy and rejuvenated when they experience humour. When was the last time that you had a good belly laugh? Have fun. If you're not currently doing this, make it a short-term goal to enjoy a fun activity at least once a week. Humour is one of the best ways to defuse a tense situation and can often calm an angry person. Remember the old saying, 'laughter is the best medicine'. For tips on humour, I highly recommend viewing these websites: www.chy.com.au/ and www.chy.com.au/books.html.

Physical

Are you caring for your body? This entails:

- eating a balanced diet

- exercising – participate in enjoyable activities to improve physical health, such as joining a gym or a sports club

- making it a priority to get sufficient sleep and rest. Listen to what your body is telling you. If you're feeling tired, fragile, emotional or vulnerable, rest or sleep, if possible

- not pushing yourself too hard. *Often, it's the NT who holds the family together.* If you don't look after yourself, mental or physical illness can result.

Intellectual

Develop your intellectual ability. Perhaps you could fulfil a dream by doing voluntary work, pursuing a career or enrolling in a course.

Mental

Taking care of your emotional well-being is imperative to prevent mental health problems such as depression and anxiety. Try to relax, enjoy life and let go of the little things (Anon NT, married to an Aspie for 48 years). Self-care is vital. Listed below are a collection of ideas to encourage self-care, adapted from information provided by ASPIA in June 2009. (See website www.aspia.org.au)

SELF

- Put self on the agenda.

- Find the right emotional distance between you and your partner that enables you to respect them.

- It's okay to be who you are, like what you like, do things you enjoy; you don't have to do only what your partner approves of.

- Create your own little space: it could be a desk, for example, or use earphones, to create a place of refuge.

- Make some quiet time for yourself.

- Find your own identity.

- Enjoy a massage.

- Have an independent income/employment.

- Enjoy pets.

- Build into your life a spiritual dimension – you may find faith and prayer of value.

- Release thoughts and feelings by writing in a journal.

- Change your own mind-set to see a problem as an opportunity to learn.
- Stop seeing yourself as the victim; see yourself as an active member of the relationship.
- Emotionally screen out negative words/actions, receive positive words/actions.
- Get your own anxieties under control (your partner may mirror your anxieties).

SUPPORT/SOCIAL

- Spend time with positive friends.
- Pre-organize support from friends, family or caring agencies to be called upon during illness or after surgery.
- Attend a support group.
- Receive personal counselling.
- Allow other people in, don't withdraw or isolate yourself.
- Re-establish social times – meeting for a coffee, seeing a movie, etc. with friends.
- Join a singing group or choir.
- Walk with friends.
- Do separate activities from your partner. Don't allow the Aspie to control how you spend your relaxation time.
- Manage phone plans to be able to afford staying in contact with friends and family.
- Help others.

ACTIVITIES

- Watch TV shows of your own choosing, enjoy comedy and laughter.
- Walk, swim, jog and exercise.
- Go on holiday with a friend.
- Do classes or a course – art, music, etc.
- Go dancing or take dancing lessons.

RELATING TO YOUR PARTNER

- Try to understand the Aspie's world.
- Allow space.
- Step back from emotional situations.
- Let some things go.
- Organizing separate sleeping/living quarters may help.
- You may need actual physical separation.
- Adjust your expectations of your partner, self and relationship.
- Try to separate the condition of AS from your partner.
- Explore your partner's perception of you: are you perceived by them as being controlling or aggressive?
- Remember that people with AS hate conflict.
- You both need love and commitment – bond with each other, in spite of it all.
- Sow seeds of suggestion, allow time.
- Give time for the Aspie to process things – sometimes this may take days.
- Allow them some time for their Special Interest.
- Realize that they understand intellectually, not emotionally.
- Have flexible plans.

Tip: Create a balance between spiritual, emotional, physical, intellectual and mental needs.

How do you replenish your energy if it's gone?

I highly recommend the book *The Emotional Energy Factor* by Mira Kirshenbaum. The author highlights many useful emotional energy boosters.

Do you have some energy in reserve for emergencies?

Maintaining high emotional energy levels is one key to survival. Enjoy at least *two* rejuvenating activities, followed by *one* draining activity. For instance, go for a walk and then meet friends for coffee. Now you have energy to do the vacuuming *or* ring a friend in crisis, *not both*. Avoiding two draining activities ensures some energy is left in reserve for unexpected illness, emergencies and the Aspie's meltdowns. Postpone tiring activities such as housework for another time, when you have more energy. It's best to take one day at a time.

Tip: Remember 'two for one': *two* energy boosting activities for *one* draining activity.

Hope begins with changing yourself

You can change more easily than the Aspie. You need to:

- be self-sufficient
- put your health needs first
- find yourself
- ensure you have enough sleep, so that you can cope emotionally, especially after your partner's meltdowns
- care about your own needs and goals
- be organized to reduce stress – employ a cleaner, babysitter or gardener, if able, or ask for help from family and friends.

What are *you* going to do for *yourself*? Start planning. Better still, start *doing* something positive now!

Take away tips

- Keep your energy cup as full as possible.
- Change your priorities.
- Look after your physical and mental health.
- Hope begins with changing yourself.
- Do something special for yourself that you've been putting off.
- Remember 'two for one'.
- Give yourself permission to say 'no'.

Conclusion

This chapter has outlined many suggestions for how to look after yourself. Decide *now*, to do things differently. Don't put it off any longer. Regain the energy required to cope with your Aspie. In order to fill your energy cup, it's vital to have sufficient sleep and do the things you enjoy. Balance and moderation in everything you do promotes good health and happiness. Looking after yourself fills your energy cup to keep you going. Now that you understand the importance of maintaining your energy, you'll be able to cope better with your Aspie. Obtaining a diagnosis of Asperger's Syndrome will be discussed in the next chapter.

The End of My Rope

A few weeks ago, at the end of my rope,
Desperately wondering how I would cope,
Tears, frustration, odd behaviour and strife,
Both have to live with Aspergers for life.

Confusion and misunderstandings every day,
That's just the Asperger's way.
Is there any hope? I am in despair.
Quiet, handsome strangers are very rare!

We've tried hard to communicate,
Since the Asperger's diagnosis date.
Learned heaps from books and 'getting in the loop'
The most helpful, joining a support group.

I learned about the 'whiteboard',
Rules inside his brain
Written in permanent ink,
That's how he does think.

His brain is different, that's all right,
Whiteboard, focus, black or white.
Withdrawal and anger are commonplace,
The solution is to give him space.

Dealing with grief,
Please give me relief.
Self-awareness is the key
To regaining my identity.

I love my husband for who he is
And the many qualities he has.
He's different, but that's okay,
Wouldn't have it any other way!

© Louise Weston (September 2007)

Chapter 4

Does A Diagnosis Help?

> *'Finding out I had Asperger's Syndrome came as a relief to me. It explained why I had trouble fitting in all my life.' (Graham Weston 2008)*

A common question amongst NTs is whether a diagnosis is helpful. Some Aspies deny having AS – an understandable reaction for someone with a diagnosis of any kind. Don't pressure the Aspie to obtain a diagnosis. Instead, gently encourage them to seek an assessment *if* they acknowledge AS traits or admit something is amiss.

At this point you may be reasonably sure that your partner has AS. The first thing to do is to decide whether or not you will share your suspicions with them. The period around the diagnosis can be extremely stressful because the frequency of meltdowns and harsh comments may increase. You may feel overloaded with information, while grieving the loss of both your identity and the dream of a close, happy relationship. This chapter explores the benefits of diagnosis, self-awareness and counselling for the Aspie and coping strategies for the NT.

Finally – an answer!

Awareness of AS usually brings a desire to learn as much as possible to understand your partner. Once you comprehend how the Aspie's brain works, this knowledge provides answers to the different way they think and behave. Sensory Integration Dysfunction (see Chapter 6) is a part of AS that may affect some, or all, of your partner's senses. When this is first realized, it gives a reason for some of the outbursts relating to food, temperature, noise, etc. You may feel relieved that an explanation exists for your partner's unusual behaviour. Finally, the light has gone on.

Change takes time

Carol Grigg from ASPIA explained in 2008:

> Most of the phone calls and emails I receive are from
> new contacts; they have just discovered that AS could be
> what is affecting their situation. Their search has become
> one of desperation as their emotional and physical
> reserves are near depletion and they're losing hope for
> the relationship, and in some cases, the whole family.
> The discovery of AS can be an exciting relief, bringing
> renewed hope and some renewed energy…for a while…
> until we realize that a magic wand doesn't exist.
>
> This part of the journey can be very dark, and it's usual
> to feel like everything we ever knew has been tossed
> upside-down and we don't know which way is upright
> anymore. The discovery of AS requires that we re-think
> the way we view everything and the way we approach
> everything within our relationship and family. On top
> of the immense effort that has already been channelled
> into surviving the situation and searching for an answer,
> this can seem beyond overwhelming. It's at this point
> [that] we need to be merciful towards ourselves and
> allow for a process to take place over time.
>
> With the search over, it's important to take time to learn
> more about AS and understand where the behaviours
> are coming from. Time gives you an opportunity to
> seek professional help for information and guidance.
> Time provides an opportunity for you to experience
> the validation that a peer support group like ASPIA
> can provide. Time will allow you to begin the process
> of healing and recovery for yourself. Time gives you a
> chance to think everything through carefully, before you
> make an attempt to introduce the possibility of AS to
> your partner, family or friends, if and when, the time is
> finally right. Time gives you an opportunity to reflect and
> to forgive yourself, releasing all the guilt you feel from not
> knowing and understanding it was a disorder. You did
> the best you could with what you knew. With time, you
> will find you can let your partner off the hook for some
> things, and you'll develop the wisdom you need in order

to know what behaviours and characteristics are harmful to yourself and the family, and that need addressing.

For the partners who've acknowledged they may have AS, change will still take time, sometimes a long time. People with AS have difficulty with change and adaptability at the best of times, so presenting to them that they've got it 'wrong' could be enough to cause a shutdown or a meltdown, and could explain a lot of the denial and hostility we experience from them. Professional guidance and supervision of this process is seriously recommended. An adult with AS won't know how or what to change. They won't have a Plan B or an alternative way of doing daily life. *Some non-AS partners have observed that as they themselves calmed down and began to quietly change their own expectations and behaviours, their partners with AS began to move towards them and develop curiosity about what was going on.* This is the kind of opportunity we all pray for – let's keep praying! (Emphasis added.) (August 2008 Newsletter, ASPIA website)

Be wise and cautious

When you start to discuss the possibility of AS with your partner, be careful and patient in the way you approach the topic. If counselling and reading marriage books were unable to help your relationship, it's understandable why you want to obtain a diagnosis quickly. It's best if the Aspie comes to their *own* realization that they're different from others.

Acceptance of AS by the Aspie aids in self-understanding, gives a reason for the frustration and other behaviours that the person experiences, and is also helpful when the couple seek counselling, as discussed in Tony Attwood's book *The Complete Guide to Asperger's Syndrome*.

The diagnosis, or strong suspicion, of AS provides the NT with reasons why the Aspie has unusual behaviours, an inability to meet the NT's emotional needs and difficulty identifying the signals that empathy is required. Some Aspies will never accept that they have AS, so don't waste your time trying to convince them.

An NT wife shared:

In some cases, the Aspie isn't interested in the fact that they may be an Aspie as they often don't see they have a problem. The diagnosis of AS is usually sought by the NT and comes as a welcome relief that you're not mad, but that an explanation exists for your partner's behaviour. When someone doesn't see they have a problem, they won't, and can't change. For an Aspie to change, it requires a massive effort on their part and all those in their life. Remember, you're dealing with a neurological, not a psychological condition. It can't be wished away, no more than you can beg an ATM machine to give out milk cartons instead of cash. You can stand there and scream at it, but it will only give out cash.

It's helpful to read some books for partners of Aspies and start living your life and fulfilling your own dreams and needs. You can't change or help to change anyone, regardless of AS or not, but you can change yourself. With this empowerment, you'll feel less inclined to care about the impact on you. Someone can only impact you if you let them.

AS is a cause, not an excuse, and some behaviours, whether AS or not, aren't acceptable. You must decide for yourself what's acceptable and what's unacceptable to you and set boundaries in the usual way. I know in my own experience, setting boundaries with an Aspie can be hard, but not impossible. My partner responds childishly and I feel bad, but I know I'll feel worse not setting them, as then I have failed myself. *The relationship I need to work on first and foremost is the one with myself.* My advice is, rather than spending your efforts making the Aspie see their ways, spend your efforts on yourself. (Anon 2009)

Carol Grigg from ASPIA wrote in 2009:

> The discovery of AS seems to have brought the clue that was missing, or removed the cork from the bottle, and many are now finding that they are beginning to be able to emerge from the tangle of confusion that has characterized their marital relationship and family life. In virtually every case, they (the Asperger partner), have not been aware of AS either and have struggled with their own confusion. Experience has shown us that once the non-AS partner is believed and validated, they are then emotionally able to explore their own issues as well. We believe that awareness begins to make the difference. Then, with the right information and support, combined with mutual

participation to find solutions, many AS/NT couples can begin their own journey towards a more mutually satisfying level of fulfilment within the relationship. This requires honesty and a desire for growth and change by both partners, not just the non-AS partner. (June 2009 Newsletter, ASPIA website)

Gently plant the seeds

If your partner becomes annoyed or frustrated due to repeated clumsiness or forgetfulness, perhaps you could gently suggest that these traits belong to AS. Listen carefully to what they say about themselves, especially if they're depressed about something that can't be helped. The best time to slowly plant seeds about AS is when your partner opens up to you.

If your Aspie asks, 'What's wrong with me?' try not to be accusatory. Instead, be empathic and speak kindly to them. A helpful reply could be, 'Nothing is *wrong* with you. I wonder if you may have AS, let's research it together.'

An NT partner stated:

When AS is mentioned, some Aspies embrace the idea and are eager to learn all they can about the reasons they're 'a little bit different'. Others are horrified by the idea and refuse to even consider it. Sometimes, you can gently lay the groundwork for them to make the discovery for themselves. At other times, even if they don't want to know about it, you'll at least know what you're dealing with and have a better idea of how to deal with your Aspie on a daily basis. (Anon 2009)

Self-awareness for the Aspie

How can someone change if they don't think they have a problem? Nagging or asking them to change won't help; instead it may turn them away. Often an AS professional needs to inform the person they have Asperger's Syndrome because the Aspie is more likely to listen to an expert. If this is done in a non-confronting, non-threatening way, they're more likely to accept the possibility of a diagnosis. This realization opens the door to change. Remember, this *may take some time*. It's best to let them change at their own pace.

One woman shared her experience:

My partner said he feels like he is missing the key to his brain and when he finds this key, it will allow him to use his brain fully. I told him that I knew what the key was and I would hate that he spend the rest of his life not realizing his full potential. So he asked me what it was and I said, 'I think you have Aspergers.'

He asked questions about it and I answered them and he said that describes him very well. I then read him some paragraphs out of Maxine Aston's book, *Aspergers in Love*. He said this is him. I explained that he was born with it and it's not curable but he can learn to live with it to his advantage. I told him about Tony Attwood and the clinic and he is keen to talk to someone to help him improve his Aspie memory and be shown a way to learn that fits his brain. (Anon 2009)

How to obtain a diagnosis

Information gathered from resources such as the internet, books, seminars and your local Autism or Asperger's association will help to confirm your suspicions. The next step is to consult a doctor with your concerns and supporting information, to assist them in making an appropriate diagnosis and/or referral. Attending a support group and implementing strategies learned can also be extremely helpful.

To obtain a diagnosis, a referral from a local doctor to a psychologist (who specializes in AS) may be required, or an individual can refer themselves to an Autism or Asperger clinic. In Brisbane, Australia, helpful organizations to approach are: Asperger Services Australia (an information and referral service) and the Minds and Hearts Clinic: A Specialist Clinic for Autism and Asperger's Syndrome. The website, www.mindsandhearts. net, lists the core criteria of Asperger's Syndrome as:

- difficulties with the ability to consider another's perspective during social interactions
- difficulty accepting change (rigid adherence to routine)
- a different sensory processing system observable by sensitivity to certain noises, lights, aromas and/or touch
- difficulty with 'reading' emotion in others and in expressing emotion appropriately
- a thinking style that is oriented toward facts, information and detail.

The importance of counselling for the Aspie

One woman shared:

> I highly recommend professional counselling from an 'Asperger friendly' psychologist. Through counselling, the Aspie can become aware of the need to change or improve the way they think and speak.
>
> Their brain may be able to prioritize thinking after some re-training from a psychologist. When a meltdown is occurring, the Aspie may become aware that something is wrong. They may not be able to control it totally, but afterwards, they can learn to try and manage what they do, and reflect more on their actions. The thinking connection is being made by the Aspie, 'Oh, I'm not supposed to do that.' They may still do it, but there has been an improvement; they're using their thinking pathway. (Anon 2009)

Coping strategies for the NT

If you're faced with the possibility that your partner has AS, talking with someone who understands the situation is vital. This may be through email, internet chat lines, phone, or personally, at a local ASD or NT support group. If you're at the end of your tether, put some of these ideas into practice to ease the burden and bring hope. Helpful strategies when relating to the Aspie include:

- Be as flexible as possible.
- Speak slowly and clearly. Aspies have trouble communicating because they may hear something different to what was said.
- Silently count to ten while waiting for an answer to a question, so they can process the information.
- Allow time for the Aspie to process ideas and emotions.
- When communicating, check that the Aspie understands what you've said. One way of doing this is to ask them to repeat in their own words what they heard.
- Don't retaliate.
- Avoid provoking them by purposefully doing things that irritate them.
- Give plenty of warning and 'scripting' prior to social activities.

- Use visual ways to communicate, for example, write social events and appointments in bright red pen on the calendar.

- Be aware of sensory issues. (Anon 2007)

- Avoid using ambiguous words like 'soon,' 'later', 'no'. To some Aspies, 'no' may mean forever. Qualify the 'no' – 'No, not now, I'll talk to you in half an hour.' (Anon 2007)

- Don't hide requests in questions, such as, 'Do you think the grass is long?' Instead, if you want an Aspie to do something, ask them using literal words, for example, 'The grass is long. Would you please mow it?'

- Avoid using statements like, 'You can help if you want to.' It gives the Aspie the option to refuse if a choice is being offered.

- Use positive statements; negative statements feed fear and anxiety. Say, 'I'm going to stay with you as long as I live' rather than 'I'm not going to leave you.' (Anon 2007)

- If your partner is in pain, sick, cranky, tired, hungry, or frustrated, avoid doing exciting or stressful things. Ignoring these *warning signs* may lead to a greater chance of meltdowns.

- Don't talk to your partner when they're getting dressed in the morning. They may have difficulty focusing on two things at once: getting dressed and listening to what you're saying.

- Aspies tend to have much deeper thought processes than NTs. Is it better to allow your partner to think things through, or create a meltdown by interrupting?

- Empathize, empathize and empathize again.

- Encourage the Aspie to pursue their Special Interest (see Chapter 14). Initially, you may not understand why this means so much to them. You may feel they experience more pleasure from the Special Interest than being with you. Try not to resent the Special Interest, rather *accept* it as the Aspie's main coping and relaxation strategy. This will lead to increased self-esteem in the Aspie and decreased conflict in the relationship.

- Allow time for the Aspie to recover from being on the computer before talking with them. If their face has a glazed look, it's possible they may still be in 'computer mode', especially after doing computer work for many hours.

- Solitude, Special Interest and distractions are effective strategies to use when the Aspie is frustrated.

- Always be prepared by having a Plan B. This works well when social or family outings are organized and something goes wrong. Thinking of another activity allays disappointment and disruption of routine, if the first plan fails.

Take away tips

- Learn as much as you can about AS.
- Plant the seeds about AS when the Aspie is relaxed.
- Recognize *warning signs* that lead to meltdowns.
- Listen and empathize more.
- Encourage the Aspie to seek help from a counsellor to deal with any unresolved issues.
- Provide space for processing thoughts and making decisions. Allow computer recovery time.
- Be prepared by making a Plan B.

Conclusion

Obtaining a diagnosis is not essential, as some couples cope quite well acknowledging and accepting AS, without a formal diagnosis. Some Aspies realize there is a problem while others deny it. Ideally, it's best if the Aspie admits they have symptoms of AS. Diagnosis can explain why they have struggled all their lives and assist you both to find new ways of relating and coping. In some countries, government and welfare agencies provide assistance. Ultimately, it's up to you and your partner if you wish to pursue a diagnosis and possibly counselling for both partners. Letting go of control is a starting point for some NTs. This will be discussed in the next chapter.

Chapter 5
Letting Go of Control

> 'We can't control the attitudes and behaviors of other people,
> but we can make right choices for ourselves.' (From p.19 of
> Choosing Forgiveness *by Sandford, Sandford and Bowman)*

Do you secretly think you can change your Aspie? You can't; you can only change yourself. Attempts to change your partner could result in issues of control slowly and unintentionally creeping in to your relationship. Caretaking or codependency could result. Are you ready to 'let go of control' and embrace new ways of relating? This chapter provides helpful hints on how to become the Executive Secretary, rather than the Caretaker.

'It's not him, it's AS'
One NT wife shared how she decided to let go of control:

After 27 years of marriage, my husband and I share an amazingly complex history, with many fond memories and a truly beautiful family. However, it hasn't been easy. In fact, it has been extremely difficult and very painful emotionally. Over the years, I longed endlessly for a close, loving relationship. I read countless books on marriage therapy and attended many self-awareness seminars and retreats. We tried marital counselling several times, with no success, until we found a psychologist who was experienced in AS.

During my marriage to an Aspie, I was dying inside, as I lost sight of myself and who I was. I used to think I'll fix the marriage first and then I'll do something for me. It should be the other way around. The most important thing was to regain my identity and let my spouse go a little bit, meaning *get my own life.* I discovered that when I met my emotional needs in other ways, I was actually *able* to let go. The tension was relieved in our relationship by allowing my husband to enjoy his Special Interest, while concentrating on my own life. Even though it wasn't the marriage I'd always wanted, I had to let go. When I increased the positives, the marriage didn't seem so bad.

My husband's unusual behaviour over an extended period of time made me realize that no matter what I did, he was going to stay the same. It finally dawned on me that all I could do was change *my* behaviour. Having a psychology background, I always felt that people could change. My Aspie husband was *totally* different; I couldn't get through to him. This made me realize that I was just wasting my time and energy, trying to save the marriage that way. I chose to *let go* and move on with my life instead of being upset all the time. If he was pleasant, I enjoyed it while I could. It seemed so simple when put like that, but it wasn't – it was a very complex marriage.

The whole focus of the marriage is different now. I've stopped trying to work out what's wrong with my husband and how to fix him. Instead, I'm pouring energy into enjoying *my* life. We have good and bad times. I try to make the most of the good times and let the bad times go. I've learned a wide range of strategies that help in our Aspie marriage, and Louise Weston has noted many of them in this book. The help that I received from the support group has given me the strength to hang in there. The group allowed me to release my frustration in a positive way and helped me to realize that I wasn't the only one in this very difficult situation.

By increasing my knowledge of AS, I now understand my husband's behaviour. If I allow him space, it makes all the difference. I finally realized *I* have to take the lead because he doesn't know what to do. I'm trying to separate the AS behaviour from the man I love. I remind myself often, that it's not him, it's Asperger's. Ultimately, the changes have to come from me.

One positive in our marriage is that I believe I've *grown emotionally*, more than I would have in an NT/NT marriage. I feel I'm a much stronger and better person with a clearer picture of who I am and what's important in life. We now have some really wonderful times, not only as a couple, but as a family. After years of grief, I'm now able to let go of the dream of the perfect marriage as I look forward to creating, with my husband, a more realistic partnership. (Anon 2009)

From this NT's experience, it's clear that letting go of control is a vital step in understanding and rebuilding your relationship. As Becvar, Canfield and Becvar say on p.13 of their book *Group Work: Cybernetic, Constructivist and Social Constructivist Perspectives*: 'Likewise, when the behavior of one person in a relationship changes and this new behavior is maintained, the behavior of the other person in the relationship cannot stay the same.' They also say that escalation of the behaviour may occur if attempts are made to change the Aspie's behaviour.

What is caretaking?

Caretaking is taking care of something that someone else is responsible for. In short, it's rescuing others from *their* responsibilities. Earnie Larsen in Beattie's book *Codependent No More* defines a Caretaker as someone who:

- finds their identity in fixing others
- can't relate to others, unless that person needs fixing
- tends to not let others grow up
- can be so focused on others that they don't take time to look after themselves
- may become exhausted trying to prevent others from experiencing negative consequences
- can be emotionally immature as adults because they've spent all their life trying to fix other people's problems. Consequently, they haven't developed other ways of relating.

When you put others first and neglect *your* needs, you can become emotionally and physically sick. Have you put your life on hold for another person? Do you consistently give more than you receive and wonder why you have no energy? Does resentment rise up within you? If the answer is yes, there could be problems with caretaking and boundaries. For further information go to: www.livestrong.com/article/14672-eliminating-caretaker-behavior/.

Codependency

'A codependent person is one who has let another person's behaviour affect him or her, and who is obsessed with controlling that person's behaviour,' says Beattie on p.36 of *Codependent No More* which is an excellent resource for more information on this topic. If codependency is an issue in your relationship, you can become so caught up in the other person's behaviour and problems that you may lose sight of your own peace of mind. The need to control your partner ends up controlling you, ultimately taking away your peace and purpose in life. Essentially, wasting time trying to rescue other people from their problems may result in neglecting yourself.

Do you constantly worry about your partner and have to know where they are and what they're doing, as well as rescuing them from the consequences of their actions? Do you tend to nag? It may be possible that you're contributing to some of the issues in the relationship. Admitting you're codependent is the first step to breaking free. Counselling is often required to assist in undoing the bad habits.

A woman married to an Aspie for 27 years shared:

> I tried everything to improve our relationship. I was totally devoted to him and always attempted to make him happy. It was a codependent relationship because he just lapped up all the attention and became even more controlling. I took his negative comments to heart for 27 years. Subsequently, I slowly died emotionally as I lost my identity and self-esteem. My health also suffered. Through understanding my husband's AS, I realized that taking his criticisms on board was *pointless and perpetually draining*. The lesson learned was: for our marriage to survive, we both had to 'give and take'. (Anon 2008)

It's important that both partners are willing to change

Aspies find change difficult because it makes them feel stressed and anxious. This is the reason why you, the NT, must be the one to examine yourself. If you've been using strategies that work effectively, then congratulate yourself and keep using them. On the other hand, if your current methods aren't working, try to *do the opposite*. Change requires moving on, forgiving and letting go of the past. It also requires self-discipline and time, and can be very rewarding.

How do you change?

Begin by identifying your strengths and weaknesses. Search the internet or library for suitable self-help books or courses that will assist with your personal growth. Read books about communication, boundaries and codependency, then practise the principles learned.

TRY TO BE FLEXIBLE

Flexibility is the antidote to the Aspie's rigid thinking and behaviour. Generally, if you try to be more relaxed and easy-going, communication will improve. It may be a slow process, but it's worth the effort.

SHOW COMPASSION

If your loved one had a medical condition, you wouldn't think twice about doing something to ease their symptoms. When trying to comfort your Aspie, remember that Asperger's Syndrome is just as valid as any medical condition.

Executive functioning

Aspies can have trouble with executive functioning, which means they may have difficulty with organizing and planning. They may forget appointments and lack the ability to change from one task to another, as pointed out by Tony Attwood in *The Complete Guide to Asperger's Syndrome*. Aspies need the NT to be their *Executive Secretary* to assist with their lack of executive functioning. This is a supportive role which is challenging, time consuming, yet rewarding.

Becoming the Executive Secretary

Some ways to assist your partner:

- being the interpreter in social situations
- finding lost items
- reminding them about appointments
- providing a low-stress environment
- giving comfort and support to decrease anxiety
- assisting with problem solving and frustration management
- providing encouragement
- helping with decision making.

You may revert to controlling behaviour

If you become overwhelmed, desperate and need help urgently from the Aspie, it's possible you may revert to previously learned, controlling behaviour. In order to cope, the Aspie may retaliate subconsciously with very difficult behaviour. They may have become used to the positive changes in the NT, when suddenly the NT's old behaviour reappears, resulting in increased anxiety and stress for the Aspie.

Give mutual respect instead of controlling

It's really important to be respectful of each other's differences. Be careful not to frivolously dismiss the Aspie's point of view. Allow them to have *their* opinion, instead of being controlling.

Strategies to facilitate change

- Review The Steps to Self-discovery and Connecting (p.24) in Chapter 1 regularly.

- Revitalize your life. The more relaxed you are, the less you'll need to be in control.

- Put notes on your mirror to remind you to avoid old behaviours.

- Avoid criticism.

- Shift the focus away from what you're *not* getting from your partner. Try to see and value the *strengths* they bring to the relationship (for more on this see Juanita Lovett's book, *Solutions for Adults with Asperger Syndrome*).

- Seek personal and marital counselling.

- Reflective journalling provides greater understanding and clarity of your partner's actions and your responses to the situations. To gain the most from writing your thoughts, it's helpful to ask yourself some questions about what occurred:

  - How do I feel?
  - Are my feelings justified?
  - Am I being too hard on myself?
  - What did I do right?
  - What could I have done better?
  - Why did this strategy fail?
  - Do I need to talk this through with someone else?
  - Do I need to talk this through with my partner?
  - What is one positive thing that I learned from this situation?

Strategies for relating more effectively

- Avoid having any expectations of your partner.

- Change the way you say things. Be clear and specific, instead of accusatory. Which sounds better? 'Why didn't you fold the washing?' or 'Can you please fold the washing so that it doesn't crease?'

- Don't criticize, for example, don't ask, 'Why are you doing that?' Aspies hate being interrogated.

- Accommodate the Aspie as much as possible by giving them plenty of space.

- Encourage them to do their Special Interest.

- Avoid complaining or interfering. Think, 'Does it really matter?'

Your partner is an Aspie, not an NT

It can take a long time to understand life through your partner's eyes.

Listen to one woman's story:

> I resisted being understanding and nice because I was thinking of him as an NT. I felt that if I was tolerant of his bad behaviour, I was *enabling* him to continue the behaviour. You can't think like that with an Aspie because their particular behaviour and thought processes demand that you treat them in a totally different way to the NT. Don't tolerate abuse; instead, be extremely sympathetic of how your partner's brain works and how their behaviour comes across. Learning as much as possible about AS is the key that helped me to understand why the behaviour happens.
>
> When I finally comprehended how very different my husband was to me, I was able to have more compassion and 'walk in his shoes'. The penny finally dropped when I realized that *he's not an NT*, he's an Aspie. I relate very differently to him now. Initially, I found this such a hard concept to accept; I fought against this for so long. I didn't accept bad behaviour from my children, so why should I accept bad behaviour from my husband? What I failed to realize was that my husband doesn't mean to behave inappropriately. Our relationship is starting to improve because *I* changed the strategies I was using and adopted new ones. It's taken me 18 months to come to this point. (Anon 2008)

Tip: Be sympathetic of how your partner's brain works and how their behaviour comes across. It's important to think of your partner as an Aspie, not an NT.

Take away tips

- Let go of control.
- Avoid complaining or interfering.
- Change can be scary for both the Aspie and the NT.
- *Remember, you can't change your loved one; you can only change yourself.*
- You might be pleasantly surprised to find that as you change, your Aspie may gradually change too.
- Avoid asking, 'Why are you doing that?'
- Make a life for yourself.
- Experiment with new ways of doing things.
- Give the Aspie space.
- Have no expectations.
- Don't criticize.
- Write a reflective journal.
- Be respectful.
- Remember that your partner is an Aspie, not an NT.

Conclusion

Learning new strategies to replace control tactics results in decreased fighting and increased energy. 'Letting go of control' means loving your partner enough to allow them to be themselves. It can be a lengthy process, sometimes taking years. Even though this is difficult, you'll be rewarded for your perseverance.

If you change your attitude and behaviour, the relationship *has* to improve. Believe it or not, it begins with *you*. Personal growth and enhanced communication is worth the effort. Letting go of control allows you and your partner the freedom to be yourselves. This promotes positive communication which will be discussed in the next chapter.

Chapter 6

Communication Strategies

*'I have a frustrating fear when I'm communicating verbally,
of not being understood, because of my inability to collect
my thoughts in an orderly fashion so I can convey my
opinions precisely and clearly.' (Anon Aspie 1996)*

At the moment, communication between you and your Aspie resembles a jigsaw puzzle. It's a very gradual process of trial and error, where you try finding ways to fit the pieces together. You may find one piece at a time and put it in the picture. The puzzle is almost finished – you think you've finally figured out the Aspie, when another awkward, strange piece pops up out of nowhere. One day a technique is effective, the next day it's not. Two steps forward, one step back.

Do you wonder why you and your Aspie have difficulty communicating and feel frustrated when you're not getting through? Many NTs identify with you. If you're willing to invest time and effort, you'll eventually learn how *you* can communicate more effectively with your partner. Numerous strategies are provided in this chapter to assist you.

Slowly implement different communication techniques

Aspies may find communicating about trivial or stressful topics unpleasant, unless it's about their Special Interest. If they're uninterested or anxious, don't persist with the conversation. If they prefer not to talk about a topic, take this as a hint and decide whether it's worth discussing at a more suitable time.

The AS/NT relationship improves when the NT slowly implements communication techniques that are appropriate for the Aspie. Although priorities and expectations will change, it's possible to learn effective ways of relating to your partner, resulting in emotional closeness.

Intuition versus learned behaviour

NTs have intuitive reasoning which means they know what to do in a difficult or unfamiliar situation and they can sense when something's not quite right. This may be a foreign concept to an Aspie because they observe facts from a scientific, instead of an emotional, viewpoint. If they practise doing what's generally expected in certain situations, several times in a row, it reinforces to them how to act in that situation when it reoccurs. One Aspie said, 'When I meet people, I remember a particular scenario and draw on that experience to know how I should act' (Anon 2007).

Adopt appropriate healthy boundaries

Communication is easier when proactive boundaries (clear-cut rules) are used. When it comes to everyday issues such as talking about the housework, don't be 'wishy-washy'. Instead, say exactly what you want, for example, you could say, 'Can you please move these items from the floor as I need to vacuum? I am giving you the opportunity to move them to a safe spot. If they're not moved by tomorrow morning, I'll need to move them so that I can vacuum the floor.' The next day, if your partner hasn't done what was asked, be consistent and follow through with the plan. I hear you saying, 'My partner will yell at me if I say that.' Let them shout. If they're upset, walk away. It's all part of the Aspie learning to respect healthy boundaries.

Define the boundaries of your ability to listen

1. Choose which battles are worth fighting.

2. Agree on a time that's suitable for both of you to discuss important issues.

3. If you're exhausted, speak up for yourself and say quietly, 'I'm exhausted. I can't listen to you right now. After I've had some time on my own, I'll be able to listen to you.' Give an accurate time-frame, for example, 'I'll be available in one hour to listen to your concerns.' Often, the Aspie will understand this. If they don't, try walking away or take time out for yourself.

The art of listening

Listen attentively

You may think you've always listened effectively. Have you wondered why you have difficulty communicating with your Aspie? Why do they say, 'You're not listening to me?' Is it because NTs are reading the signs of an impending meltdown and planning what to do, instead of actually paying attention and listening to what's being said? It's vital that you listen intently to your partner. Nodding and giving verbal feedback are some of the signs that show you're paying attention. How well do you listen? Consider the following questions honestly.

- Is the TV turned off?

- Are you doing something else while listening?

- Is the environment free of distractions and interruptions; for example, is the phone off the hook?

- Is your mind focused on what your partner is saying? Be honest here. Are you thinking of all the things *you* must do?

REALLY LISTEN

One female NT shared:

> After reading *Living and Loving with Asperger Syndrome* by Patrick, Estelle and Jared McCabe, it finally dawned on me that I had to listen, *really listen* to my partner. This means, instead of switching my brain off when the frustration episodes start, I need to figure out *why* my Aspie is becoming frustrated, by *listening* to *what* he's saying. It's been difficult to stop asking questions and using 'unintelligent words'. I put a sign saying this on my mirror to remind myself. When he's explaining every little detail about something, I listen until he's finished speaking. I only ask a question if absolutely necessary. I have to tell myself, 'Don't ask questions' (even if I'm desperate to know something). Sometimes, I've patiently waited for up to half an hour to clarify what he said. An example was when he was telling me (in extreme detail) all the facts about the computer he bought, including accessories and software programs. I've noticed that if I try and interrupt, he gets that frustrated look on his face and either says blunt and harsh words or has a meltdown.
>
> When I read Estelle's dilemmas as described in *Living and Loving with Asperger Syndrome*, I could totally relate to her; especially on *listening* to frustrations for what they are, instead of being angry with my partner for

being frustrated. I like the way Estelle shared how to decrease stress: answer questions exactly the way presented, with a yes, or no, and think before you speak. (Anon 2008)

Avoid asking questions

Aspies really dislike being interrupted by questions while concentrating or analysing their thoughts. Sometimes, questions are required to obtain your partner's opinion on something. Try to decrease the frequency of unimportant questions.

An NT wife shared her story:

One day shortly after diagnosis, I was out of bed before my partner. Every morning, I like to discuss the plans for the day. This particular morning, I asked him how he was feeling. He said, 'All right, until I saw you.' This comment shocked me. I then asked, 'What would you like to do today?' He became very annoyed. I thought people with AS prefer to be prepared in advance so that they're aware of what's expected. My partner wasn't interested in chatting about what was happening for the day. He said that I was badgering him. (Anon 2008)

Tip: Don't ask two questions at once and sometimes avoid asking any questions at all.

ASPIES MAY FEEL PRESSURED TO ANSWER

Asking questions can put an Aspie on the spot to think of a quick answer. Also, talking and interacting when they're already overloaded could increase their stress levels. If an Aspie is asked, 'Did you like the party?' they may have to think about the appropriate response. At the same time, their thoughts prior to your question may not have been resolved. Reacting in a cranky manner may result from feeling pressured to answer quickly or to carry out your request, as well as being drawn away from what they're focused on. Is it any wonder your partner gives a delayed or angry response?

USE POSITIVE WORDS

If you use positive words at the beginning of a sentence instead of threatening or negative ones, it's more likely that you'll receive a good response from your partner. A word such as 'let's' is an inviting word suggesting cooperation with another person. The secret is how the question is asked. The statement, 'Let's go out for dinner' doesn't need a 'yes' or 'no' answer. Instead of having to think of a long-winded reply, the Aspie could perhaps just say, 'OK'. Compare the statements, 'Let's go out for dinner' and 'Would you like to go out for dinner?' The first is a statement whereas the second is a question. For the Aspie, 'Would you like to…' might require extra analysing of thoughts such as 'Am I hungry? I'm a bit tired. If I go out, I'll need to have a shower. Oh, and then my partner might expect me to meet their emotional needs.' Is it any wonder that Aspies snap back at NTs?

Inviting words or phrases include:

- Is it possible for you to…?
- Tell me about…
- Perhaps we could…
- Tell me more…
- May I…?

Barriers to effective listening
Sensory Integration Dysfunction

This is a disorder involving unusual perception of sensory input, where Aspies may have problems with tactile defensiveness, auditory abnormalities and taste aversions, as Ashley Stanford discusses in her book, *Asperger Syndrome and Long-Term Relationships*. Aspies may speak loudly when they experience a strong aversion to any of the five senses: smell, taste, sound, touch or sight. Regulating temperature and interpreting pain can also be difficult for an Aspie. They may be able to see, smell and hear things that you can't, due to a heightened perception of sensory stimuli. Consequently, your partner may react to things out of the blue, which can leave you feeling drained and shocked. If too much (hyper) or too little (hypo) stimulation occurs at once, they may go into sensory overload, resulting in a meltdown.

Sensory overload can be overwhelming for the Aspie, making it quite difficult for them to listen attentively. While communicating, part of a sentence or its intended meaning may be missed. This can lead to an argument because the Aspie might have misinterpreted the message. Conflicts can be reduced if you empathize with your partner and make an effort to decrease or avoid the sensory overload issues that irritate them.

HELP YOUR PARTNER AVOID POTENTIAL SENSORY OVERLOAD

Don't expect your Aspie to attend parties or large gatherings. Some may enjoy these activities, while others won't. Allow them the freedom to choose whether or not to attend. Aspies also have difficulty concentrating during a conversation due to sensory overload, especially when more than two people are in the room. Crowds and noise intensify sensory overload, subsequently increasing stress levels. As a result, symptoms of AS such as frustration, anxiety and anger intensify, increasing the likelihood of a meltdown. NT partners shared their stories:

Story A: Too much noise

One day, shortly after diagnosis, I was trying to see life through his eyes. We went to the Main Roads Department to hand in our old car rego plates. It was a very noisy environment with lots of people, in addition to the radio and loud speaker blaring. I said to him, 'It's loud in here. Is that annoying you?' He said, 'Yes, times that by 30 and that's what I have to deal with every day.' This helped me to really *empathize* with my husband, as well as begin to understand what he must go through. The magnitude of what Aspies have to cope with hit me hard. (Anon 2007)

Story B: Too many people talking

One night, we were at a friend's house and there were five people talking at once. I asked my husband to pass the salt and he yelled at me. On reflection, I realized he raised his voice due to sensory overload because too many people were talking at once. (Anon 2007)

Difficultly understanding the message
A. VERBALS AND NON-VERBALS

NTs listen to verbal information in conjunction with assessing body language, for example, the person's behaviour and facial expressions are interpreted at the same time. On the other hand, Aspies may not notice the non-verbals because they're *focusing on the person's mouth*, which is discussed in Tony Attwood's book *The Complete Guide to Asperger's Syndrome*. If your partner is stressed, they may have difficulty maintaining eye contact and picking up non-verbals simultaneously, because they're trying to concentrate on *what* you're saying.

Tips: Don't force eye contact. Communicate while giving your partner a massage or tickling their back. Another suggestion is to enjoy a favourite relaxation activity together, without looking at each other.

B. ASPIES MAY TAKE LONGER TO PROCESS OR ANALYSE INFORMATION

Your partner may take up to ten seconds before they respond to a question. When stressed, the response time is likely to be longer. If you're oblivious to this fact and keep talking, communication difficulties can arise due to the Aspie being overloaded with information. You might talk 'ten to the dozen', while they're still processing the first sentence. This is probably why Aspies are so quiet because they're analysing their thoughts before they speak. NTs can learn from this admirable and positive Aspie trait.

Tip: Allow extra time for your partner to digest information, analyse the pros and cons and respond to your instructions.

C. DIFFICULTY HEARING THE MESSAGE

Misunderstandings can occur as a result of the Aspie or the NT missing vital information. This can be especially difficult if you're trying to converse while physically in different rooms. Discuss important issues with your partner when you're alone together in a quiet room with minimal distraction.

How to communicate with Aspies
Learn to speak 'Aspergese'

Aspies have concrete ways of viewing things, meaning everything is either black or white. 'Aspergese' means speaking the Aspie's language. According to Tony Attwood in his book, *The Complete Guide to Asperger's Syndrome*, this can become second nature to the NT as they use their own unique method of helping the Aspie interpret daily issues. Some ways of speaking 'Aspergese' are speaking clearly, being consistent, trying to 'think like an Aspie' and using new communication techniques.

A. SPEAK LOGICALLY

Approach and respond to situations in a logical manner. Use phrases that work such as 'that's illogical' or 'that's not common sense'. Some helpful examples explaining money issues are provided:

An NT shared:

> I wanted to employ a cleaner because I had a new baby and was exhausted. I tried to convince my partner that this was needed but he wouldn't listen. After advice from another NT, I explained it logically to my partner by writing down the cost, duration, benefits and what I would sacrifice. This worked. He agreed immediately. (Anon 2009)

Another NT shared:

> When the Aspie is concerned about the finances, explain in a logical manner how the bill can be paid. For example, if it costs $600 to service the car and he states this is expensive, add the amount spent on the car maintenance for one year and divide the amount by 52 weeks. If the total is $1000, this works out at $19 per week to maintain the car. This is a realistic figure. He might back down from the shock of a large bill if you break up the total car costs over one year. (Anon 2009)

B. SPEAK LITERALLY

What is your partner's preferred way of explaining their point of view? Listen carefully to the words used when they communicate. It takes effort and can be difficult at times to see the Aspie's 'black or white' perspective. One NT explains below how her husband uses 'Imagine this scenario' to explain a situation. Now she uses these words to explain her point of view to him:

> Imagine your investments. You put money into them and they grow. That feels good, doesn't it? Imagine that our relationship is an investment and every time you give me a compliment, your investment grows. It makes *me* happy which makes *you* happy. It's a win-win situation. He liked that! (Anon 2009)

Make no assumptions: say exactly what you mean

NTs often make requests in a 'not-so-straight-forward' way, in order to be polite. This causes confusion for Aspies. Say what you want and how you want it. If a kiss and cuddle are needed, say that. Don't expect your partner to know what your needs are, as this may be foreign to them. If you don't tell them what you want, you may not receive it. For more on this see Juanita Lovett's book, *Solutions for Adults with Asperger Syndrome*.

Avoid confusing words or sarcasm

One NT wife shared:

> Sometimes, on bad days, I would try sarcasm on my husband, saying things like, 'You're a *really* hard worker' or 'You look after me *so* well.' The funny thing was that he would often take me literally and be quite pleased with himself.
>
> However, one day he said, 'Sometimes, I think you're being sarcastic. I'm often not completely sure but I just get a feeling that you're being mean towards me.' I tended not to use sarcasm very much after that because I realized I was hurting him. (Anon 2009)

Ask the Aspie to tell you 'what' to say

One woman commented:

> My husband was having a go at me and wasn't able to articulate. He wanted me to do something the *right* way. I said, 'I'm struggling with this. You tell me *exactly* what you want me to say.' That shocked him for quite a while. Eventually, he turned to me and said: 'This is the way I want you to say it, "I know that you've had a really long and tiring day and that you're exhausted. After you've had a rest, I would like you to help me with the dishes."'
>
> I repeated these words exactly. Using this technique worked well, preventing further communication problems. (Anon 2008)

Gently plant the seeds

Listen to one NT's story of how she encouraged her Aspie to go on a holiday:

> My husband likes to have time to carefully consider the pros and cons before we do anything, so he can make the final decision himself. Tactfully making suggestions over a period of one or two weeks works well. If suddenly bombarded with information, he immediately says, 'No'. Typical examples include:
>
> • Next month would be a good time to take a holiday; the weather is usually fine then.
>
> • The beach and the country are both good options.
>
> • Some great value holidays are advertised in this week's paper. I'll leave it here in case you want to have a look.

• When you're ready we can check them out on the internet.

Together, we look at the selections and choose one. To go on holiday is the priority, so I'm just happy we've made a decision. (Anon NT, married to an Aspie for 48 years)

Effective and proven communication methods
Practical and visual

- Compile a list of household chores and prioritize in order of importance.

- Show the Aspie how to do tasks in specific ways, qualifying what you want and how you want it done. *Providing a detailed, written description works well.*

- Rather than repeatedly describing what you need, show your partner the exact item that you're talking about. 'Show and tell' – don't just tell.

- Use *In the Zone Charts* (see Chapter 9).

- Write down an equation or draw a picture on a piece of paper to explain how important your needs are and compare it to a second equation or picture, which includes your partner's Special Interest. An example:

  - Plenty of affection = a happy wife.
  - Taking photos = a happy hubby.

- Make a deal or contract. Most Aspies understand 'tit-for-tat'. You could try to make a deal like, 'If we do the chores together today, we can do something fun tomorrow.' If the Aspie asks you to do something, you could use the same principle, for example, 'Sure, I can do that, if you help me with this first.'

- Use their Special Interest to explain concepts.

Listen to a success story:

Fishing is his Special Interest, so I likened my bathroom accessory purchases to him catching a big fish. I said, 'You know how you get really excited when you catch a big fish? That's how I feel at the moment because I want to make the bathroom look really nice.' He understood how much this meant to me! (Anon 2009)

Verbal

- Use 'I feel' statements instead of 'You make me feel' statements, as described in Mandy and Anne Kotzman's book, *Listen to Me, Listen to You.* 'I feel' statements are less threatening and are an assertive method of communication.

- Avoid bombarding the Aspie as soon as they arrive home. Allow them to recover from *their* day before you talk about *your* day.

- Speak slowly and clearly in a calm, rational, business-like manner.

- Avoid giving multiple instructions simultaneously because the Aspie may have difficulty remembering them all. Instead, give one request at a time, for example, say: 'Please grate the carrot.' When this task has been completed, you might say, 'Now, please cut the cucumber.'

- Give the Aspie a maximum of two choices.

- Keep communication brief and to the point. Aspies may find it difficult to cope with lengthy conversations.

- Be specific when you communicate. Say, 'I really need you to…' Or, 'I would like you to…' Or, 'You need to…'

- Use the 'broken record technique'. An example is, 'We'll talk about it later,' or 'I'll let you know in the morning' (Anon NT, married to an Aspie for 48 years).

- Use non-statements, words that are noncommittal. You're not saying 'no' and you're not saying 'yes'; for example, try: 'That could work.' These statements acknowledge that you've heard what the other person has said (Anon NT, married to an Aspie for 48 years).

- Always be kind in the way you speak to the Aspie. Listen to the tone of your voice when you speak. Use 'thoughtful requests' instead of 'selfish demands', as talked about by Willard Harley in his book *Love Busters.* An example of a thoughtful request is, 'Please take the rubbish out and put it in the bin.' Some examples of selfish demands are:

- 'I just wish you would hurry up and hang that washing out.'
- 'You never do anything for me. Why are you lying down again? Can't you help?'

- Another option is to link the desired behaviour to the current behaviour. For example: 'As you go out the door, please take the rubbish' (Anon 2007).

- Give *genuine* praise often. Aspies prefer honesty. One NT praised her husband for cleaning out the gutters. He replied happily, 'I love it when you praise me' (Anon 2009).

- If the Aspie does something wrong, don't make a big deal about it. Let it go (Anon 2007).

- Don't contradict your partner.

Listening

- *Really* listen to what's troubling your partner.

- Ensure you understand what the Aspie says and vice versa.

- Be sensitive to your partner if you suspect that they're deep in thought. There is more on this in *Alone Together* by K. Bentley. Giving them space may reduce misunderstandings.

- Explain to your partner that if they don't tell you what they're thinking, you can't read their mind.

- Be precise when asking the Aspie about their day. The statement, 'How was your day?' could confuse them, as it may be taken literally. One Aspie stated, 'What part of the day are you talking about? Do you mean the lunch break, the meeting I told you about or the traffic on the way home? Be specific by stating *exactly* what part of the day you're talking about' (Anon 2009).

Take away tips

- Aim to talk only when you're both in the same room.

- If possible, be aware of and decrease sensory stimuli.

- Listen attentively.

- Allow the Aspie time to process or analyse information.
- Use visual methods to communicate.
- Use phrases such as 'illogical' or 'that's not common sense'.
- Say exactly what you mean (speak with intent).
- Speak the Aspie's language (speak literally).
- Ask the Aspie to tell you what to say.
- Use the Special Interest as an example.
- Ensure you understand what your partner says and vice versa.
- Make a deal or contract.
- Remember to show, rather than tell.
- If exhausted, arrange another time to communicate.

Conclusion

If you're new to the concept of AS, it's likely that many of the old ways of relating aren't working. By making a consistent, conscious effort to use different communication techniques, there will be a decrease in the frequency of meltdowns. If you feel like you're holding the relationship together, try implementing successful strategies presented in this chapter. Some partners who put these suggestions into practice noticed a significant improvement in their relationship within two days (Anon 2009).

It's obvious you need to guide your Aspie in this confusing world of misunderstandings and sensory overload. Learning to speak 'Aspergese' is a high priority in improving communication with your partner. Thinking like your partner so you can understand them will assist with interpreting emotions. This will be discussed in the next chapter.

Chapter 7

Helping Your Partner Interpret Emotions

'The Aspie doesn't have a clue about emotions or what
the NT goes through.' (Anon Aspie 2009)

Emotions play an important part in any relationship. Both partners in an AS/NT relationship need to understand that Aspies and NTs interpret emotions differently. Do you ever wonder why your partner has difficulty empathizing and understanding feelings and emotions? Do you long to be understood? Stories in this chapter shed light on the difficulties Aspies experience regarding empathy, anxiety and emotions.

Empathy

Empathy involves 'putting yourself in another person's shoes', being able to imagine what another person is feeling, and trying to understand exactly what they're going through. Aspies have difficulty knowing when empathy is required and picking up emotional signals, especially during times of stress. This is described by Carter, who used a brain scanning technique called positron emission tomography (PET) to diagnose what's happening in the brain. It highlights the areas that are in use at a particular time and within a specific context. Carter used PET scans on Aspie and NT subjects. The test results revealed that Aspies were trying to understand another's behaviour using logic, rather than empathy. Therefore, it usually took longer to process the answer when empathy was required (as Maxine Aston explains in her book *The Asperger Couple's Workbook*).

It can be concluded from the above that if Aspies take longer to pick up the signals when empathy is required, they could have trouble deciphering feelings and emotions. Aspies see things logically, whereas NTs view the emotional and logical content of a situation. Consequently, it's possible that the Aspie may miss the 'big' picture.

An Aspie comments about empathy:

I'm unaware that I've hurt other people's feelings because I believe that my 'empathy circuit' is faulty. The wire that's supposed to be connected to the empathy circuit is connected to the anxiety circuit in *my* brain. When I'm normally supposed to be feeling empathy, a signal is sent off to my anxiety circuit. I already feel anxious. Then I experience anxiety 'Bang! Bang!' twice in a row resulting in withdrawal.

As an Aspie, I come to a point in a relationship where I become very hurt. I try to explain to my NT partner how hurt I feel but they don't understand, so I withdraw. Then I just give up trying. I still hang in there because that's better than experiencing total loneliness again. Having no one in my life causes me to withdraw even more. However, having someone always in the background suits me because it's better than having no one at all. (Anon 2008)

Difficulty with empathy

One NT wife shared her story:

At about 8 p.m. one night, I had excruciating stomach pain and vomiting. My husband had to wake up at 4 a.m. for work, so I reassured him that I would be all right and that he could sleep in the spare room. After he went to bed, the pain and vomiting increased, so I rang my mother to ask if she could drive me to the hospital. My husband was woken by the noise of me vomiting. He was shouting at me and had a very distressed look on his face. I couldn't believe he was ranting and raving, when I was in so much pain. Our teenage daughter helped me with my slippers and dressing gown. We looked at each other in disbelief as he continued to yell at me. Our daughter said, 'Dad, can't you see that Mum is sick?'

The shouting increased when he found out that my mother was driving me to hospital. He rang her and managed to speak more politely, clarifying that he would drive me to the hospital. I'm not exaggerating when I say he yelled all the way there. In a calm voice, I said, 'Please stop yelling, I'm really, really sick.' All I needed was some empathy and sympathy. I didn't have the energy to say I needed some tender loving care. Thankfully, he stopped yelling when we arrived fifteen minutes later. I was admitted to hospital with appendicitis. This situation made me realize that something was very different about my husband. (Anon 2008)

The above scenario can be a common experience for the NT. Sickness or pain in others often increases the Aspie's anxiety, due to their feelings of helplessness, loss of control and difficulty picking up the signals when empathy is required. Often, a meltdown can result.

Tip: If unwell, confide in an empathic, caring friend for comfort and support.

It's extremely difficult for the Aspie when you're sick

When the NT's role of Executive Secretary is threatened by illness, this causes disruption to the Aspie's routine and precipitates several changes. They may have to run the household or help with the children. This change in routine can cause them irritation and annoyance, increasing the stress they're currently experiencing.

Your partner may have trouble dealing with the changes and not be able to sense when empathy is required. They may seem uncaring and anxious, when in fact they simply don't know what's expected. Also, if you're sick, the Aspie may become anxious because you're not looking after *their* needs. If *you're* not coping, be careful not to blame it on the Aspie.

Ideas of what to do if you're sick

1. Lower expectations of the Aspie temporarily. Always be ready to implement Plan B in the case of a crisis or sickness.

2. If you're in the middle of a great deal of unavoidable stress, don't expect the Aspie to be there for you. Most often, it's quite the opposite. Their behaviour deteriorates as *you* become more anxious.

3. You may feel like you're never going to come out of this nightmare, especially if you're working and looking after young children. Hold on to hope. Ask for help from family and friends. A supportive network is imperative; it takes some of the pressure off you, enabling a quicker recovery.

4. Put yourself first. Lower your expectations regarding household chores and social activities. Also consider temporarily hiring a cleaner, gardener and a babysitter or nanny.

5. If working, take some leave, if possible, to regroup and recover your lost energy.

6. Do everything possible to become well and regain energy. It's vital that your physical and emotional energy are restored, so that you can maintain your function as the Executive Secretary for your partner.

Theory of mind and mind-blindness

Tony Attwood in his book *The Complete Guide to Asperger's Syndrome* describes theory of mind as 'the ability to recognise and understand thoughts, beliefs, desires and intentions of other people in order to make sense of their behaviour and predict what they are going to do next' (p.112).

Mind-blindness is an *absence* of theory of mind. This is discussed further in Chapter 14. In *Asperger Syndrome and Long-Term Relationships*, Ashley Stanford states that this is, 'the inability to see others as having their own state of mind' (p.273). Tony Attwood, in *The Complete Guide to Asperger's Syndrome*, talks about a typical five-year-old being able to observe social cues, and figure out what they mean and what to do. It can take some Aspies 30 or 40 years to understand social norms and that other people have minds. Aspies experience anxiety and feelings of uncertainty because they may be unsure of what another person is thinking or feeling. Comments from NTs:

- My husband is in his 50s and doesn't understand that I have feelings and opinions (Anon 2009).

- My partner wasn't aware that others had a mind until he was 36 years old (Anon 2009).

Emotions

Remember, your partner's brain is wired differently to yours. On p.130 of *The Complete Guide to Asperger's Syndrome*, Tony Attwood states that 'Aspies have a structural and functional abnormality in their amygdala, a part of the brain that helps perceive and regulate emotions such as fear, anger, anxiety and sadness.' This is the reason for their inability to recognize and control emotions. Subsequently, communication problems can be a regular occurrence.

Aspies may describe emotions as either 'good' or 'bad' feelings, but are unable to discriminate the subtle nuances and shades of feeling like NTs intuitively can. Aspies are often not aware of whether 'feeling bad' is jealous, afraid, sad or depressed or whether 'feeling good' is happy, relaxed, satisfied, in love, etc.

Confusion about what's expected

When it comes to reading emotions, Aspies become confused about what's expected of them. They may feel uncomfortable when other people around them are emotionally needy. On the other hand, if they could identify a practical, logical solution to your problem, most Aspies would help immediately.

Tip: Give the Aspie a practical task to do instead of expecting them to meet your emotional and social needs.

Aspies share their stories
KNOWING WHERE I STAND AND WHAT'S EXPECTED IS REALLY IMPORTANT

Everything has to be black or white, meaning straightforward and uncomplicated. I need to know where I stand and what's expected of me. Many Aspies give up communicating with their partners because they realize it's impossible to relate on a level that the partner understands. (Anon 2008)

I DON'T EXPERIENCE MANY EMOTIONS

I don't know that emotions exist so I'm unaware of what I'm missing. If someone points it out to me, I get it. I might not know how to express myself, so I watch what works for others and continue doing that. I don't experience any real emotion or feeling. I just know that if I do this, I'll get a certain reaction from another person. When the person responds positively, I figure out that the person must like me; therefore everything I'm doing must be okay. As an Aspie, I've got no idea about love. The emotion, if I ever experience it, is probably nothing compared to what NTs feel. I haven't got a clue what NTs go through. I'm glad I'm not an NT. I couldn't cope with all that emotional tension. When someone dies, all the sadness you go through. You poor people! (Anon Aspie 2008)

ASPIES FIND IT DIFFICULT TO COPE WITH THE HIGHS AND LOWS OF EMOTIONS

Feeling elated is such a rare emotion that I don't know what to do with it. The feeling is so foreign, so strange, it creates anxiety. Some Aspies may decrease this anxiety through substance abuse or an addiction of some kind. Being elated is as bad as being anxious. The Aspie may be ecstatic because he has finally been able to reach a goal. Either extreme of emotion creates anxiety; really depressed or really elated. There must be an even keel. I can't cope with highs or lows; I must always be in the middle of the emotional scale. (Anon 2008)

Why do Aspies become exhausted?

Aspies can find interpreting facial expressions, emotions and non-verbal gestures draining. In social situations, a significant part of the exhaustion results from constantly trying to understand other people's emotions. They work extremely hard trying to remain undetected, due to the pretence that must be maintained in order to provide 'suitable' emotional responses.

When an Aspie has spent a lengthy time with people, they might not be able to handle further communication with others for the rest of the day. They express this through their body language and behaviours including collapsing on the bed, a 'phased look', or covering their head with sheets or pillows. Try to keep this in mind by not expecting your partner to notice whether you're sad, angry or tired, when they arrive home from work or a social event. It's best to allow one hour or more for your partner to unwind in solitude before bringing up emotional issues. The exception, of course, is emergencies.

Not there emotionally for you?

When you need your partner the most, they may not be emotionally available for you. During times of crisis, pain or extreme sadness, you may experience feelings of isolation, lack of support and understanding. Many NTs know exactly how you feel, especially the longing for your partner to be there emotionally for you. The Aspie may want to help you but be unaware of what to do to provide comfort. If you crave emotional comfort, avoid interrupting your partner when they're focused on their Special Interest. Instead, talk to a trustworthy, empathic and caring friend.

Tip: Develop support networks. This could prevent resentment towards the Aspie for not always being emotionally available.

Teach your partner what to do

During an unemotional time, explain what you need your Aspie to do next time you're emotional. Some ideas that work are to:

- tell your partner that you need a hug when you're crying
- give them a practical task to do, such as make a cup of tea for you
- ask them to listen, rather than offering advice
- remind them to make you feel special next time you're upset, for example, 'buy me flowers' or 'tell me how much you love me'
- create peaceful surroundings, for example: ask them to take the children out to give you a break or play your favourite CD, etc.
- write notes that describe clearly what you need them to do, for example: 'if I'm crying, do "x".'

Interpreting emotions for the Aspie

In reality, you probably interpret *for* your partner most of the time and then attempt to share your interpretation with them.

This is one NT's story:

> One evening, I was busy in the kitchen when the timer started beeping. My husband came into the kitchen, agitated by the noise. Sensing his frustration as he looked through the pantry, I asked him, 'What's wrong?' In a loud voice he stated, 'I don't know, maybe I'm hungry.' I asked whether the anxiety of commencing a new job the following day and the noisy timer might be the cause of his irritation. He agreed. As we prepared dinner, I asked him to do one thing at a time. Later, as we ate, I was silent so he could reflect on the cause of his agitation. (Anon 2008)

Tip: By asking the Aspie to do one thing at a time, stress is reduced, allowing them to focus on emotions. If possible, allow times of silence.

Holding down my emotions (beach balls)

One Aspie shared:

> I have several emotions that I'm trying to control at once. It's like trying to hold several beach balls under the water simultaneously. I deal with one

and suddenly another comes out of the water and I must hold it down. The emotions are connected to underlying life issues that I haven't dealt with yet. I'm trying really hard to deal with them by holding as many beach balls under the water as possible. This isn't my NT partner's problem so I shouldn't become angry at her. I'm angry at myself for not being able to juggle several beach balls all at once. (Anon 2009)

Feelings

Feelings are the emotional and physical sensations that accompany an emotional reaction. It can be distressing for an Aspie when they have to describe their feelings to others (Anon 2009).

Don't ask an Aspie how they feel

One Aspie shared:

If I'm already overloaded and you ask me a question, I almost explode because I'm still analysing what's happened for the day. If you ask, 'Are you angry?' you've just asked me to process why I would be angry. I think, 'Where did this come from – why would I be angry?' It makes no logical sense. Why would I be angry, when I'm standing here concentrating on preparing dinner? I'm chopping my carrot and concentrating really hard on what I'm doing. Then, all of a sudden, a change in routine and a shift of the thought processes occurs because someone comes right out of left field asking, 'Are you angry?' The look on my face doesn't mean I'm angry. It could mean something completely different. (Anon 2009)

Why the blank look?

In situations where others would be expected to display strong emotion, an Aspie may have a blank look on their face. This doesn't necessarily mean they're sad, depressed or even upset. The blank look may betray their real feelings within or might not mean anything at all. As NTs, we presume something is bothering the Aspie, when in actual fact we may be making a big deal about nothing. To them, a blank, unresponsive gaze may be normal.

One couple were discussing facial expressions. The NT was distressed by the look on her husband's face and said, 'Are you angry?' The Aspie replied, 'No, I'm not angry; don't tell me how I feel. I can't help the way I look' (Anon 2009).

Tip: Often, Aspies don't know *how* they feel so an NT can make matters worse by *asking* them how they feel.

Anxiety

Aspies often experience anxiety with symptoms including chest pains, stomach pains, palpitations, headaches and sweaty palms. Your partner may not know what anxiety is, especially if they've been experiencing the symptoms for years. To them, these symptoms may be normal as no one has informed them otherwise.

Aspies may not notice if an NT is anxious

If Aspies are often unaware of their *own* anxiety and frustration, they may be unable to identify anxiety and frustration in others. They may become anxious when they're required to meet another person's needs or when empathy is expected. Your partner may become stressed and frustrated due to their inability to 'put themselves in your shoes'.

FEELINGS OF HELPLESSNESS

If your partner does notice your emotions, they may experience an overwhelming feeling of helplessness; they might not know what to do. In a close relationship, stress, whether good or bad, can influence the intensity of these feelings, resulting in confusion. Aspies can become physically and emotionally exhausted due to a constant state of anxiety and the effort it takes to process information. Is it any wonder that conflicts occur when Aspies and NTs have different perceptions of feelings and emotions?

To recap, Aspies may experience anxiety when:

- empathy is required
- they feel that they don't live up to the NT's expectations
- socializing is expected, whether pre-warned or not
- in a new situation
- change occurs
- they have multiple stressors to deal with simultaneously.

TO MANAGE ANXIETY, ASPIES LIKE TO FEEL IN CONTROL

Due to problems with anxiety, Aspies need to feel in control. During a crisis or emotional situation, an Aspie may experience increased stress due to diversion from their structured routine. They have a need to feel in control as this:

- decreases their stress levels
- maintains order/routine (if interrupted, a meltdown can ensue)
- helps them to cope.

Stress affects Aspies by:

- decreasing their ability to understand and interpret emotions
- increasing their confusion
- decreasing their ability to concentrate
- causing difficulties with communication, hindering their ability to relate.

Why doesn't the Aspie get it?

Listen to one wife's experience:

> One day, I was in a bad mood, feeling exhausted from lack of sleep. Fed up with living with an Asperger, I was thinking to myself, 'He doesn't care; he doesn't get it, why doesn't he get it?' It would be nice if he could understand me for just one day. Life would be much easier if he could figure out when I'm drained and realize the times when I need a hug. (Anon 2008)

Aspies are not going to 'get it' very often. It's quite possible that your partner may never fully understand you. Acceptance is essential. You need to:

- develop more realistic expectations
- snap out of the pity party
- look after yourself
- focus on the Aspie's positives
- be their interpreter
- love them unconditionally
- meet your own needs.

Deal with a crisis on your own

Generally, we're not like typical families where the partners support each other and work together during a crisis. An AS/NT relationship is different, due to the Aspie having great difficulty coping with stress.

When a crisis occurs, the Aspie may lose control and have difficulty managing, let alone comforting others who are emotional. A calamity may send an Aspie into red zone. The NT is simultaneously coping with the predicament, while comforting their partner. Does this sound familiar?

Do you often feel exhausted and burnt out from putting your emotions on the back-burner? If you try to keep your energy cup at least three-quarters full and have no expectations, things will start to improve. Refer to Chapter 3 if you need new ways of regaining energy.

Take away tips

- Remember, Aspies have difficulty understanding emotions and empathy, especially during times of stress.

- Give the Aspie a practical task to do instead of expecting them to meet your emotional needs.

- Aspies see things logically, whereas NTs view the emotional *and* logical content.

- Don't ask an Aspie how they feel.

- Due to problems with constant anxiety, Aspies need to feel in control.

- If unwell, confide in an empathic, caring friend for comfort and support.

- A supportive network is imperative.

Conclusion

At times you may feel angry, frustrated and upset with the Aspie; they're probably feeling the same way. Perhaps you could guide your loved one in this world of confusing emotions by being their interpreter. In order to reduce stress, you need to be adaptable, while showing empathy and patience towards your partner.

Emotions can be difficult for the Aspie to fathom. When you and your partner are communicating well, gently teach them what to do next time you're emotional. Work on being understanding and helpful, instead of being critical. It may be difficult, but it's worth the effort. Sometimes, a really close moment can be shared.

Experiencing constant anxiety and difficulty interpreting emotions can increase stress and add to communication problems in your relationship, resulting in blunt, hurtful words from the Aspie. Strategies to cope with these words are discussed in the next chapter.

Chapter 8

Surviving Blunt and Harsh Words

Quick recovery begins with refusing to listen to harsh words, staying calm and walking away. The sooner you do that, the faster you'll recover and maintain your energy.

Harsh comments from anyone can be difficult to deal with, even more so when they come from your partner. It can feel unbearable and extremely draining when you're constantly devastated by 'blunt and harsh words'. Many NT partners describe their Aspie's abrupt words in this manner. This chapter provides strategies to decrease the frequency of these words and outlines methods of resolving conflict. It also describes quick recovery time which is one of the vital keys of connecting.

What is 'quick recovery time'?

Quick recovery means *immediately* dealing with the emotional pain caused by the Aspie's blunt and harsh words. This is done by *refusing* to accept these words, forgiving often and quickly and moving on with your day. *Staying calm* decreases the frequency of blunt and harsh words. Also, *walking away* from the Aspie puts an end to the conflict.

The stories below illustrate the importance of 'quick recovery time'.

Story A

Early one Saturday morning, shortly after diagnosis, my Aspie husband said, 'The marriage is over. I can't cope with this relationship any more.' We went from a great relationship to that statement out of the blue. Harsh words are draining. I tried to be strong and pretend it didn't hurt, keeping it together for about an hour. Then I went to another room and sobbed and sobbed, being careful that he didn't see me cry, because I thought it would upset him.

Later that morning, when we were out shopping, I felt an overwhelming exhaustion come over me as a result of the morning's events. When we arrived home from the shops, he said, 'I think I will just move out when our son moves out. It will be easier on my own; actually I think we should just get divorced.' This floored me! I thought, 'He can't mean this, we're getting on so well.' I was extremely upset that he'd mentioned divorce.

That afternoon, our friends were due to visit for lunch. Not feeling very sociable and suffering from sheer exhaustion, I said, 'Honey, I'm going to have a rest, can you please prepare the lunch?' I spoke literally because that's the language he understands. When our friends arrived, I was still in bed.

My lovely NT friend came into the bedroom to see me. She intuitively knew that something was wrong. When I told her why I was sad, she said, 'He obviously didn't mean it because he's in the kitchen talking about going on a cruise with you when you retire.'

Shocked that he could forget such strong and hurtful words, I tried to put it behind me. Since then, I've learned to ignore harsh comments. He doesn't usually remember what he says anyway. One way I cope is to think, 'He can't help it and he doesn't mean it.'

In hindsight, giving him a job to do (preparing the lunch) worked really well. It stopped the 'energy battle' from getting worse because I didn't engage in a fight and he was able to focus on something. (Anon 2010)

'Quick recovery time' is vital

For the NT in the above story, quick recovery time was essential for her sanity. She needed to *regain emotional strength* before the guests arrived for lunch. Knowing that her partner required space, she retreated to the bedroom to gain desperately needed rest. Although still exhausted when their friends arrived, she felt less emotional after recovery time.

If 'quick recovery time' is not put into practice, it can take up to three days or longer to recover from blunt and harsh words or meltdowns. On the other hand, regular use of this method decreases recovery time because you don't take the words to heart as much. It's inevitable that you'll still feel hurt from abusive words, but walking away and regrouping lessens the blow. With practice, it becomes easier to deal with the words.

An accumulation of blunt and harsh words that are not dealt with just compounds and causes health problems or a blow-up later!

Story B

The following couple were renovating their home; the NT wife needed her husband's assistance due to a limiting physical condition. The Aspie didn't tell his wife the 'whole truth' about his planned Special Interest.

The wife shared:

My husband came home from a very long and tiring day enjoying his Special Interest.

I said to him, 'Can we put the fence up next weekend?'

He said, 'No, I won't be here next weekend.'

I said, 'I beg your pardon. You're going away next Sunday, not the *whole* weekend.'

He said, 'No, I'm going away for the whole weekend.'

Well, I nearly went through the roof, I could feel my blood pressure rising. I said to myself, 'Stay calm. Stay calm.' Instead of retaliating, I said to my husband, in a calm, firm voice, 'Hang on a minute. Let me get this straight. You're going away for the whole weekend.'

He said, 'Yes, didn't I tell you?'

I said, 'No, it's written on the calendar that you're going on Sunday, not Saturday.'

He said, 'No, I'm going away for the whole weekend, so I won't be able to do the fence.'

I kept telling myself to stay calm as I said to my husband, 'Well, if that's the case, let's quickly do some jobs around the house now because there won't be any time next weekend to do them.'

This statement and the opportunity to actually do some chores together gave me some time to think. I didn't mention to him how upset I was. After the jobs were done, we had a really nice meal together.

The next day, when he was quiet and in a good mood, I discussed boundaries with him in a calm, firm voice. The significance of warning me he was planning on going away and for how long was also mentioned. I said that it would help if he was mindful of the family's needs by checking if it was reasonable to spend the whole weekend doing his Special Interest.

Generally, I've found the secret to quick recovery time is to avoid making a fuss if my Aspie hurts me. If you make a fuss and become angry, they may go berserk. However, if you can quickly recover from the words that they've hit you with and wait for a better time to talk, you feel less drained and the outcome is far more successful. (Anon 2009)

The woman in the above story has learned vital strategies: stay calm, speak clearly and quietly, and use distractions. She made a 'win–win' situation out of a bad situation by stating firmly: 'Let's do the jobs now.' As a result, not only did she have a 'willing worker' but her husband stayed calm because *she* stayed calm. By focusing on the jobs, this gave her time to think, rather than reacting and becoming upset. She focused on the positives rather than the negatives, resulting in chores being completed.

NTs can sometimes find Aspies' behaviour infuriating. If you react in anger, whatever you do or say lacks credibility. You have to be the role model, the example. If the Aspie sees you upset, they may lose control. Aspies mirror behaviour, good or bad. Don't expect them to apologize. They may never do that, especially at the point of a meltdown. If you push them to say sorry or even talk to them during a meltdown, their behaviour may escalate, making the situation worse.

Tip: Be a good role model for your partner. Try to remain level-headed at all times.

Possible reasons for Aspies speaking harshly
No warning signs preceding emotions
As mentioned in the previous chapter, Aspies don't always experience pre-warning regarding emotions like NTs do. They may be annoyed, anxious, agitated, frustrated, angry, or all five at once. One Aspie said, 'It's all or nothing. I'm relaxed or stressed, calm or angry, nothing in between' (Anon 2009).

Mind-blindness
Remember, Aspies may not be able to see your point of view or know that you have needs. If you're unaware of this, you may become annoyed or retaliate, potentially causing an explosive response from the Aspie, resulting in blunt and harsh words.

Facts before feelings
Aspies may be unaware they've hurt people's feelings by using blunt and harsh words. The need to point out mistakes is a common trait of Aspies

to the detriment of others' feelings. This point is explored further in Tony Attwood's book *The Complete Guide to Asperger's Syndrome*. This can be very upsetting for the person being criticized. These episodes become easier to cope with once you realize the Aspie usually doesn't mean to be offensive.

Tip: Teach your partner the importance of being sensitive to other people's feelings. Sayings that could be useful in the household are: 'feelings before facts' and 'people come before the project'.

High standards for themselves and others

One Aspie shared:

> It's all about high moral standards that I set for myself. Guilt, depression and anger can become a major problem when I don't live up to these principles. If I can't always follow my own moral values, I'll always be angry. To me, it's black or white. I've broken my own moral standard. I think I'm a failure. Doing the right thing by sticking to this standard is my highest goal. Nevertheless, I'm spiralling downwards as I struggle with the compounding negative feelings triggered by my sense of failure. A vicious cycle of pessimism and unhappiness eventuates which is one reason why I snap at my partner.
>
> Suddenly, two weeks later, I realize, 'Hey, I'm not breaking my moral standards as often; I must be doing all right.' When depression, anger and guilt lift a little, I know I must be doing okay. One month later, I think, 'Hey, I'm doing really well. I'm not breaking my moral standards at all.' Contentment and happiness are achieved, leading to increased self-esteem and acceptance.
>
> I don't need antidepressants because I'm not depressed. It's black or white. After a few weeks, if I did feel sadness or depression, the feelings can lift really quickly. I'm either depressed or not depressed. It's not logical to be depressed. (Anon 2009)

Tip: Encourage the Aspie to follow their morals, values and beliefs.

A strong sense of social justice (social policeman)

An Aspie's story:

> I have a strong sense of social justice. If I do or see something morally or socially wrong, I can be extremely angry at myself or at what I see. It's black

or white. Neither myself nor anyone else should go against these values. This guilt or annoyance leads to crankiness all day, a heightened level of anxiety and anger directed at myself or other people for not meeting the moral standard. Hence, I'm most likely to be in orange zone *constantly*. If my partner, or children, say one little thing out of place, I can explode with frustration and anger, sending me into red zone (see Chapter 9). I can become aggressive in nature with rage taking over, leading to emotional and physical abuse. If alcohol is added to the situation, the problem is exacerbated. (Anon 2009)

Substance use (or abuse)

It may be more difficult for the Aspie to understand the NT when alcohol is in their system. A recovered alcoholic said it takes several days to rid the body of alcohol and the mind of unrelated unclear thinking. Subsequently, relationship issues arise and irritability, withdrawal and physical illness can become a vicious cycle.

An Aspie stated:

If the problems with anxiety and substance use continue, the Aspie may not grow emotionally and socially – it can stunt their growth in these areas. Aspies are already socially inept; alcohol can bring about more isolative tendencies, thereby increasing communication difficulties in the relationship. It can take several months to improve relationships after giving up addictive substances. Aspies have enough trouble relating in a sober state, without adding a mood altering substance. (Anon 2009)

Methods to reduce blunt and harsh words

Don't forget the importance of speaking in a *calm and respectful* manner to your Aspie. If you've tried several techniques and nothing seems to work, don't lose hope. Remember, if it's taken years for the relationship to reach this point, it could take a few years to repair the damage. *Silence or ignoring hurtful words* often works. It doesn't mean giving the 'silent treatment' for days or weeks; this, too, is a form of abuse. You may wonder how it's possible to ignore what another person says to you. It takes practice and is at times still hard, even for partners who've known about AS for years. We're all human, after all. If you know the Aspie is in orange zone, *giving space* really helps. If this is ineffective and they follow you or continue to berate you, despite trying the above techniques, the next step is either to walk away or say, 'I'm going to walk away now, but I'll be happy to speak with you when you're calm.'

Walking away protects both partners

Do you walk away when your partner berates you? This can be really difficult to do at first. Somehow, it doesn't seem natural. We may have been taught by our parents that it's rude to walk away when another person is speaking. Perhaps it's ingrained into us to stand up for ourselves? It's important *not* to engage in fights or take blunt and harsh words personally. Retaliating is the worst thing you can do – more on that later. Implementation of this technique (walking away) on a regular basis makes it easier. Remember what the NT shared in Chapter 1– the earlier you walk away in the conversation, the more likely frustration meltdowns will decrease. Once this concept is understood and implemented, it's possible to experience peace and happiness.

Don't escalate the situation. Avoid blaming the Aspie, regardless of it being their fault. When you're in the wrong, apologize. When you're in the right, don't prolong the argument. The Aspie is less likely to react to silence. After the encounter you might be pleasantly surprised, especially if they apologize. They are more likely to open up later than to blame you. Walking away defuses the situation, shows thoughtfulness and protects everyone in the household. Allowing your partner space invites them to draw closer to you, helping to stop the cycle.

Separate the Aspie from 'Aspie behaviour'

After the initial hurt from the harsh words, reassure yourself and realize that this is simply typical Aspie behaviour. When you're vulnerable, it's difficult to separate your partner from their behaviour.

Construct a logical argument

Do you have difficulty with your partner often wanting to be right or have the last word? When the Aspie is adamant that they're right, try to avoid arguing with them. Instead, logically explain your point of view. An Aspie and NT couple shared their thinking:

THE NT'S PERSPECTIVE

When the Aspie insists that they're right about something, *construct a logical argument* that proves your point. As Aspies have problems relating to feelings, they can have difficulty understanding you, especially if you're emotional. On the other hand, when facts, rather than emotions, are presented, you have a greater chance of helping them understand your point of view. (Anon 2010)

Tip: When constructing a logical argument, always remember that mind-blindness needs to be taken into consideration.

THE ASPIE'S PERSPECTIVE

Your Aspie may like to put the shaving can on the bathroom window ledge because it's easy to reach. Rust forms on the bottom of the can due to water splashing on it, resulting in staining of the window ledge. Nagging the Aspie to put the can away in the cupboard will fall on deaf ears. A better way to explain the reason for putting the shaving cream away is to explain *logically*, 'The rust from the bottom of the can is discolouring the paint on the ledge. If this continues, it could cause a future maintenance problem, requiring unnecessary work and extra money.' (Anon 2010)

Tip: Explain your perspective by showing the facts in a *logical, business-like manner*, verbally, visually or in written form.

How to stop the 'chasing and withdrawing' cycle

Don't pressure the Aspie for anything. Be aware: the more you want and need them, the more pressure you put on them, leading to a repetitive cycle of 'chasing and withdrawing'. Consequently, the NT is exhausted and the Aspie retreats into withdrawal or shutdown mode, hindering communication even further.

AVOID CRITICISM

If an Aspie is stressed and someone criticizes them, they may go into defence mode and say something extremely hurtful to the offender. The sad thing is that they may not even realize that they've hurt your feelings, remember what was said, or even notice that you're upset or emotional. To make matters worse, you may waste precious time and energy running after them, hoping for an apology or a connection. If you start condemning your Aspie they may withdraw further. Try *not* to run after them. Stop the cycle of 'chasing and withdrawing' now.

AVOID SELF-PITY

If you see yourself as always being the victim of rejection, with a 'poor me' mentality, it can be difficult to move on with your life. Staying in this mind-set hinders personal growth and the ability to accept that your partner is an Aspie. If you choose to stay in this negative position, the chances are that you'll become needier, especially if you think your partner doesn't love you. Now you're in an endless, futile cycle of rejection.

Tip: Try to change the mind-set which tells you that you're continually being rejected.

AVOID RETALIATING

When a statement is said against you out of the blue, it's natural to be offended. The remarks, whether true or not, are often said because the Aspie is extremely frustrated. Avoid retaliating. It's ineffective as it only escalates the situation. Verbal and physical abuse is unacceptable. After an episode, an important step is to try to figure out the context of the outburst, while maintaining safety for you and your family. When your partner is in green zone, try discussing the situation and what triggered the event. It's possible to remove yourself from this relationship 'merry-go-round'.

Have empathy

As mentioned in the previous chapter, empathy is required when trying to assist the Aspie with handling their emotions. Empathizing may help decrease the frequency of blunt and harsh words.

Use proactive boundaries

Don't react to your Aspie's defensive comments. Speak clearly and in a firm voice when you set boundaries. Remember, proactive boundaries are clear-cut rules. Most Aspies like rules as it helps them stick to their rigid routine.

This is what one NT said to her Aspie (18 months after AS was realized):

'I understand that things are stressful at work and that you're really tired but that's no reason to take it out on our family when you arrive home.

It's not our fault that you're feeling this way. Do you understand what I'm saying? I see that you're stressed but you mustn't take it out on us because we haven't done anything wrong. If you take it out on us, it alienates us further from you. Trust me; you need us at the moment.'

He understood this because I've proven to him that I'm not his enemy. I've made him feel emotionally safe. It's taken longer than a year. By backing off and being gentle, yet firm, with my boundaries, we've drawn closer to each other. Also, I've entered into his world. I've *disconnected emotionally* by looking after myself, becoming centred and whole. My physical and mental health has improved. With a healthy emotional distance, I was able to empathize with him more and work through the grief of the loss of the dream marriage. Our relationship is much better now because I've found myself and have strong boundaries. I can now reconnect with my husband. The number one priority is making sure that *I look after myself.* (Anon 2009)

In the above story, the wife used proactive boundaries and some of the strategies found in this book. She is now happier, not only with her own life but with the huge improvement in her AS/NT partnership.
Try statements like:

- Please don't speak to me that way.

- Do you realize that the way you're speaking to me is very aggressive and upsetting?

- It's unacceptable to speak to me that way.

Encourage the Aspie to maintain a structured routine

Once again, remember, no expectations = no disappointments. Avoid overloading the Aspie with too many chores. Don't expect them to listen to you and do things the way *you* believe they must be done. Reducing stress in the household as much as possible is one way to help your partner keep a structured routine, which decreases the chance of blunt and harsh words. Try not to interrupt the Aspie when they're intensely focused on something and explain the importance of this to other family members.

Conflict resolution

Use Maxine Aston's three rules of fair fighting, as noted on p.42 of her book, *The Asperger Couple's Workbook*, 'no physical abuse, no verbal abuse and no bringing up the past'. Remember, it's unfair to restrict and be manipulative with your partner's Special Interest. Instead, encourage them to pursue it.

Why do Aspies have difficulty resolving conflict?

The Aspie may:

- be experiencing sensory overload issues

- show less remorse, compared to NTs. One NT shared, 'My husband rarely apologizes. He lacks remorse' (Anon 2009)

- be unaware of alternative ways of resolving conflict, so revert to immature methods like 'emotional blackmail or inflexible adherence to their own point of view', as described by Tony Attwood on p.119 of his book *The Complete Guide to Asperger's Syndrome*. Listen to two Aspies' comments:

  - 'The only point of view is *mine*. Why argue with you, when you won't come over to my way of seeing, believing or doing it?' (Anon 2009)
  - 'I don't need to resolve conflict' (Anon 2008).

No wonder couples are struggling in AS/NT relationships! It's clear from the above points that, once again, it's up to you to take the lead, speak calmly and try to resolve the conflict.

Tip: Don't force your opinion. Instead, allow your partner to come around slowly to your point of view.

Respect your partner

In a relationship that has been damaged through a significant amount of conflict, partners often start to disrespect each other. Once the hurt begins to heal, the importance of *mutual respect* becomes apparent. It's really important that *you* change your response to conflict because some Aspies don't see the need to resolve conflict. As an NT, you're aware that others have their own point of view. Perhaps you could attempt to discuss the pros and cons of the argument with your partner. Both partners need to respect the other person's desire to resolve, or not to resolve conflict. Perhaps a compromise can be reached? This doesn't mean that you necessarily have to agree with your partner's view, but respecting it is really important.

Tips to resolve conflict with your Aspie

- Stay calm and patient to gain respect from your partner.
- Be careful what you say and try not to accuse.
- If they seem frustrated, don't approach them, unless it's an emergency.
- Be gentle, loving and forgiving.
- 'Agree to disagree.' Quit fighting over the little things. It wastes time and energy. Sometimes, it's appropriate to agree or simply ignore the little things.
- Give your partner a job to do as a distraction.
- When relating to your Aspie, avoid the behaviour that *they* display. If they're domineering, do the exact opposite: avoid controlling, nagging or bossy behaviour.
- Avoid becoming involved and bothered by their denigrating words, accusations or impossible demands. Often, when they make an accusation about *you*, they're mirroring what *they're* feeling:
  - If they're stressed, they might accuse you of being stressful to live with.
  - If they're controlling, they may accuse you of being controlling.
  - They might say, 'You're so critical,' when they're the one criticizing.

Strategies to cope with blunt and harsh words

- Prayer.
- Use the 'NT filter technique' to listen. This involves visualizing funnels connected to your ears, with a sieve on each end. Listen to the facts and respond to the person after the comments have been through the filter. Hurtful, inappropriate, derogatory or untrue words are filtered out. This might sound silly but it works. By the time you finish imagining the words being filtered, you've calmed down enough to respond to the facts of the message.

- Emotionally detach, with love, by ignoring the Aspie's harsh words. Instead, focus on looking after yourself and maintaining your energy, by resting or re-energizing. A relaxing day out without your partner can be very uplifting and rejuvenating.

- Take their comments with a pinch of salt and be emotionally strong and confident in yourself. If you're happy with yourself, the Aspie's words won't affect you as much, especially if you know they're untrue. Ignore their negative comments by replacing them with positive thoughts about yourself. This lessens the emotional pain which drains your energy. Some things really don't matter, so let them go.

- Develop a calm, relaxed attitude towards life. Take some deep breaths whenever you feel stressed or anxious. This helps you to stay calm.

- Ensure you receive adequate sleep.

- Let go of the dream of the perfect relationship.

- Praise yourself out loud often – it's good therapy, for example, 'I'm doing a great job.'

- When feeling down or having a bad day, think, 'It doesn't matter,' 'They don't really mean it' or 'They can't help it.' One NT shared: 'These statements work wonders every time. They help me to keep going and have a bit of a laugh' (Anon 2008).

- When your partner begins to enter orange zone (see Chapter 9), use distraction techniques to help them calm down.

Self-esteem enhancers

Always remember you're a worthwhile person, despite what your partner says about you. Say positive affirmations aloud to yourself or put notes on the mirror as a reminder. It's important to look after yourself and maintain your self-esteem. Put the past behind you and start living *now*. Some ideas of how to increase your self-esteem:

- Engage in a revitalizing activity alone.

- Read inspiring books.

- Listen to uplifting music.

- Enjoy nature and animals.
- Call an empathic friend.
- *Don't* feel guilty when you do something for yourself.

Take away tips

- Distance yourself from the Aspie.
- Avoid dwelling on negative comments.
- Have adequate sleep – things always seem worse when you're tired.
- Avoid retaliating.
- Give the Aspie something to focus on.
- Ignore harsh comments.
- Try not to interrupt the Aspie when they're stressed.

Conclusion

At the moment, you may feel like the relationship is going backwards and you're 'drowning in quicksand'. Please, don't give up hope. If you and your partner are willing to make an effort, it's possible to have a happy relationship.

Start today by changing the way *you* respond to the Aspie's comments. Remember, quick recovery time means refusing to listen to hurtful words, staying calm and walking away. This results in the ability to deal more effectively with meltdowns; an extremely important topic discussed in the next chapter.

Chapter 9

Coping with Meltdowns

'We cannot change another person's behaviour but we can change the way we deal with it.' (from Jane Verity's workshop paper, Positive Approach to Difficult Behaviour)

Does your partner struggle with aspects of daily life that you take for granted? Try to put yourself 'in their shoes' and gently guide and encourage them when they're distressed. Frustration is one of the most difficult symptoms your partner must face. Listen to an Aspie's comment: 'For the Aspie, it's a world of untold, confusing and frustrating misinterpretations' (Anon 2009).

In this chapter, you'll discover some reasons for meltdowns and ways to prevent them, as well as techniques to decrease their frequency. *In the Zone Charts* are useful tools which outline ways of predicting meltdowns, as well as providing successful strategies to assist in calming your partner.

Why does a meltdown occur?

In *The Complete Guide to Asperger's Syndrome*, Tony Attwood explains that an Aspie may experience a meltdown due to difficulty in regulating emotions. Other factors that result in meltdowns are stress, sensory overload, difficulty reading emotions and communication problems. Meltdowns result if too many stressors occur at once. A frustration meltdown is where an Aspie moves from green or orange to red zone in a few seconds.

One Aspie said to his NT partner:

You have a highway of pathways to run your thoughts through. I only have one little street which becomes clogged with thoughts because the little gate can only hold so many thoughts. Then the gate opens and I explode because too much is happening in my life. (Anon 2009)

Meltdowns are a fact of life

You can't fix meltdowns but you can control how you respond to these stressful events. Avoid feeling responsible or guilty for the meltdowns. Each individual is responsible for their own actions and reactions. Ultimately, a step in the right direction is accepting the inevitability of your partner's meltdowns.

Tip: If you alter *your* response to situations by not reacting in a negative way, your Aspie could also alter *their* reaction.

In The Zone Charts

My husband and I have developed *In the Zone Charts* to use during times of stress and frustration. The charts found at the end of this chapter consist of three colour zones: green, orange and red. Possible triggers, behaviours, strategies and relaxing activities are described.

First, green zone is *relaxed* zone where the Aspie is quiet and stress-free. This is most likely to occur when they're pursuing their Special Interest. Orange zone is *warning* zone, where symptoms of stress or overload are building and the Aspie may show signs of being agitated. Finally, red zone is *danger* zone, where the Aspie has exploded or 'phased out'. This is the 'point of no return'. If you must interrupt the Aspie when they're in orange or red zone, do so with care. Examination of what meltdowns are and why they occur is important before viewing *In the Zone Charts*.

Frustration can lead to meltdowns

Frustration is the state of being unfulfilled or dissatisfied, especially when presented with difficulties that can't be overcome. Aspies *constantly* have to deal with anxiety and sensory overload, coupled with clumsiness and forgetfulness. Is it any wonder that these factors lead to feelings of annoyance, disappointment, irritation and exasperation? Your partner may also experience feelings of resentment, due to not being understood or accepted by others. Add all these factors together and a meltdown can occur. Keep reading to find out what *you* can do to help minimize your partner's frustration. Let's look at some causes of meltdowns.

Exhaustion

For Aspies, time spent socializing may need an equal amount of time in solitude as an energy restorative (personal communication with Professor Tony Attwood in 2010). It's important to try to prevent a meltdown by not bombarding your partner as soon as they arrive home. Aspies use *all* their emotional strength to deal with every minute of the day. This means that dealing with people, in conjunction with numerous sensory issues, drains them of energy. After a long day, they're deflated and have nothing left to give the NT. An Aspie can be likened to a rubber band. If stretched gently, it slowly comes back into shape, but if the rubber band is stretched beyond capacity, it breaks. Aspies can only take so much sensory overload, anxiety, change and stress in one day, before they snap. On arrival home, they need to release tension gradually. *Their home is their haven.* If you provide relaxed surroundings and have an easy-going attitude, it's more likely that the Aspie will gradually ease their way back, instead of snapping like a taut rubber band. Their mind needs time to readjust and recover from the day. Before they can even start to consider other people, they need time to ease back into shape like the rubber band. After a rest and enjoying their Special Interest, the Aspie will most likely respond better to demands.

Tip: Encourage your partner to have an afternoon sleep or rest.

Memory loss

When Aspies are in a stressed state, in orange or red zone, their memory is more likely to fail. They become frustrated when they lose things. The item may be right in front of them but they can't see it due to sensory overload. Through *maintaining your composure and speaking quietly*, you can assist your partner to calm down, while you look for the lost item. The Aspie can also become annoyed with themselves when they forget information. The example below illustrates the struggles that Aspies have with memory issues on a regular basis.

One NT shared:

One morning before I went to work, he was upset about something he read in a book. I said, 'Don't let it wreck your day; forget about it and move on.'

He said, 'Yeah, I will probably forget about it when you go to work.'

Five minutes later, I was ready to drive off when he said, 'I have a vague idea I was cranky about something. What was I angry about?'

I said, 'It doesn't matter.'
I thought to myself, 'Could he be joking? Surely he hasn't forgotten about it in five minutes!'(Anon 2007)

Tip: Don't ridicule or make fun of the Aspie if they're forgetful.

Clumsiness

In *The Complete Guide to Asperger's Syndrome*, Tony Attwood explains that balance and coordination may be difficult for Aspies. Bumping into furniture, dropping items, spilling drinks and having difficulty catching balls are embarrassing and frustrating examples. In an effort to prevent clumsiness, Aspies may speak their thoughts out loud to remind themselves to concentrate, so that they're less likely to be clumsy. Sometimes, it can seem like their frustration is directed at you, when in actual fact they're annoyed at themselves.

Reaction to change

Aspies have difficulty with the slightest amount of change. 'Acquiring something new or doing things differently creates a feeling of excitement or anxiety that's hard for me to handle' (Anon Aspie 2009). Changing your appearance, for instance, having your hair coloured may be hard for them to accept. Prepare the Aspie for changes by explaining how and why things will be different if 'x' occurs. Avoid environmental changes like moving or throwing out their possessions as this can be very traumatic for them. 'Environmental routine' is discussed further in Chapter 10.

If multiple changes occur around them, the Aspie may experience a delayed response due to difficulty coping with stress. Sometimes it may take them several days or weeks to process an event. Either suddenly or gradually, depression can set in and lead to withdrawal mode. A preventative measure is to have a structured routine for the Aspie. If people annoy them or disrupt their routine, they can become very angry, instantly going into red zone. The episode may last from five minutes to a few hours and can be forgotten quickly. Meanwhile, you're left picking up the pieces, smoothing things over…sound familiar?

Interruptions

Your partner can become acutely distressed when asked to leave the point of focus to do something else. If their train of thought is interrupted during a crucial part of a project, they may explode in frustration as they *can only focus on one thing at a time.* Aspies hate being interrupted because it takes too much effort to concentrate again, recoup motivation and tune in to the project. Put yourself 'in the Aspie's shoes' for a moment as you read the example below.

THE OLYMPIC GAMES

Imagine you're watching your favourite Olympian swimmer on TV and he's winning the race. The atmosphere is electric; the fans are cheering loudly and the announcer is becoming more excited by the minute. Your swimmer is coming home; it's neck and neck as they close in on the finish line. You're waiting with bated breath to see if your Olympian wins. At that crucial moment, a black-out occurs. The sound equipment fails, the lights go out and you're left wondering whether they won or not.

AN ASPIE'S PERSPECTIVE

In the above scenario, the NT is left feeling disappointed as the anticipation of the final result is lost. This is similar to how an Aspie feels when you pull them away from their Special Interest. They are torn between the pressures to see your request through, versus the need to see the finished results of their own little world. This is how an Aspie often feels in a relationship with an NT: pressured and torn between two loves. (Anon 2009)

YOUR PARTNER MAY 'PERCEIVE' YOU AS DEMANDING

If the Aspie is preoccupied with their thoughts and the NT interrupts them by asking them to do something, the Aspie may interpret this as the NT being demanding. Difficulty processing thoughts may be bothering your partner, not the behaviour of others around them. The best rule here is to avoid interrupting the Aspie when a significant event, to them, has occurred. Obviously, you can't mind-read everything that's going on inside their head or always know when to talk and when to be quiet.

Tip: Don't take it personally when the Aspie yells at you or says that you're demanding.

Little irritations

The slightest irritation can seem enormous to Aspies. Remember, *little* things about themselves and others can irritate them much more than they bother you.

NT's perspectives of frustration episodes

Story A

One day when we were driving home from a long trip, I said, 'I need to go home and get my book to post.' He said, 'Don't do that – let's go straight to the local shops.' I said, 'Okay, can you post it for me tomorrow?' He said that would be all right. Later that afternoon, I showed him the book and the piece of paper with the address written on it. I explained which post pack to buy, etc. He became very annoyed with me, stating loudly, 'If I knew all this was going to be involved, I wouldn't have offered to do it.' I just ignored him and carried on with what I was doing. (Anon 2008)

Story B

One day about a year ago, my Aspie and I had been travelling for two hours in the car. He was driving and had to contend with the usual stress like road works, traffic and other people's reckless driving. I was chatting away when he said loudly, 'Will you shut up?' That's not usually how he speaks to me. He's polite to others, unless he's frustrated. I didn't know my talking was bothering him. Instead of expressing his annoyance, he waited until he was *really* stressed to tell me. This situation helped me realize that my partner becomes irritated if I talk too much, especially if he's overloaded and frustrated. I learnt that when he's driving, I need to be quiet. As a bubbly NT, I become bored very quickly, especially if I can't talk. One useful strategy I've found is listening to music through headphones, while a passenger in the car. (Anon 2008)

Prevention of meltdowns

Try not to have an extremely busy schedule, especially when the Aspie is juggling multiple stressors. If you're stressed, they're stressed and a snowball effect occurs: a meltdown is likely to ensue. Avoid anger if possible, as it inflames the situation. If the Aspie does something that upsets you, the choices are to retaliate and become angry (which will send them into a meltdown) or *stay calm* and turn the situation around to your advantage. The latter is the best option. If your partner senses that you're trying not to be angry and you're working on being calm, this will be appreciated and they may be more approachable and willing to talk.

Seven ways to prevent meltdowns

Experiment with the following techniques to see which strategy is most effective for you and your partner.

SOLITUDE AND SPACE

Aspies require *ample space* after feeling overwhelmed or overloaded from the events of the day. They find people emotionally draining and need to have a sleep or enjoy their Special Interest to refill their energy cup (see Chapter 3).

The following are some stories from NTs about giving space:

Story A

Sometimes, as often is the case in a relationship, I need to ask my partner a question about finance, children or even plans for relaxation. I find that if I logically and intelligently give information to him and leave him alone for 15–30 minutes, saying, 'Have a think about that. I'll come back later for a chat', communication is far more likely to be successful and an agreement reached. (Anon 2009)

Story B

My husband was burning off some bush on our property. He became very intense in what he was doing. I went to see how he was getting on and to discuss the plans for the day. Instantly, I could tell from 'the look' (anxious, nervous, blank stare) on his face that this was a 'no go' zone. The more I talked to him, the angrier he became. So I jokingly said, 'Well, I'll just go and play in the bushes for a while.'

An hour later, I came back and tried again. He was very serious and engrossed in what he was doing. I said, 'You're doing a great job.' My husband was still scowling. Prior to learning about AS, I would have badgered him about the plans for the day. Knowledge of AS has taught me not to attempt to plan the day when he is focused and has a scowl on his face. (Anon 2007)

Tip: When the Aspie is absorbed in something, it's pointless talking to them because they may not be able to think about something else at the same time. They need their space.

MAINTAIN A CALM AND STRUCTURED ENVIRONMENT

- Stay calm and remain easy-going.

- Allow the Aspie to have their structured routine where possible, because this gives them stability and security.

- Encourage your partner to slow down the pace by resting or relaxing, doing their Special Interest.

- Offer to teach deep breathing exercises when anxious.

- Be structured in your family routine.

- Try not to be too emotional as this increases their anxiety.

- Use silence.

- Avoid telling them how they feel as this may be interpreted as controlling.

- Introduce soothing techniques or effective stress relievers such as firm massage or light tickling to the back, arms, legs and feet. A 'squeeze' massage works well to calm them when stressed. Ask your partner to lie on their back and instruct them to take deep breaths and concentrate on their breathing. As they breathe out, use both hands to gently squeeze a section of their body. Start from the head and continue down one side of the body, finishing with their feet. Do exactly the same to the opposite side of their body, starting with the head again. One Aspie enjoyed this massage and commented, 'It's comforting, like that "squeeze machine" that Temple Grandin invented' (Anon 2009).

- Suggest participation in anger management or emotion awareness courses. It may be helpful to attend together so that you can support each other.

- Encourage the Aspie to undertake physical exercise to release their frustration.

DISTRACTIONS

A distraction is something that takes away attention from the issue at hand, or a method of diversion like praise, a surprise or a form of entertainment. Distraction techniques can help to deflect the Aspie when heading towards a possible frustration meltdown. Experiment to see what works for your relationship or try some of these ideas: massage, play a fun game, cook your partner's favourite meal or discuss their Special Interest. One way to 'change the topic' is to be spontaneous, for example, you could say, 'Let's go to the movies' or 'Let's go and buy an ice cream.' Can you think of other distractions?

An NT's story:

Prior to going to our friend's house for dinner, my partner was in 'withdrawal mode' and I was depressed and exhausted from 'walking on egg shells'. Despite how terrible I felt, I still went. After dinner, I was looking through my friend's newspaper to see if any cars were for sale. As we needed to buy a new car, I distracted my Aspie from 'withdrawal mode' by showing him the cars that were for sale. It worked. He was happy again and the new Special Interest was to buy a car. (Anon 2007)

HUMOUR

When an Aspie is distracted by humour or diversion, anxiety may be decreased.

An NT wife shared her shopping story:

My husband and I are in our 50s. Neither of us likes shopping together as it can end up in meltdowns. The other night we had to go shopping for toilets because we are renovating our home. Both of us were tired, so I knew it would be a little stressful looking through hardware stores at toilets. My Aspie husband was also cranky and cold so I prepared him for the unpleasant weather and night ahead by ensuring he wore warm clothing. He loves food so I said, 'Let's eat some yummy food first and then go to the shops.'

I decided to make a game out of it by running up and down the aisles, being really silly. Laughing together, I kept opening up the toilet lids and throwing paper in them. Even though it was fun, we couldn't find what we wanted. I noticed that I was starting to become upset and emotional because I was exhausted, so I said to him, 'I'm so over this, how about you?' He agreed.

In previous years, I would have kept pushing to finish the shopping until I'd found the item I was looking for, but now, I knew it was time to go home. It turned out to be a fun night, with both of us acting like a couple of teenagers. It could have been really awful if we weren't light-hearted and relaxed. I really think humour is an excellent way to relate better to your Aspie. (Anon 2008)

SPECIAL INTERESTS

Aspies enjoy being in their own little world, exploring, focusing on and pursuing their Special Interest. They feel relaxed and excited when they discover fascinating and unusual facts to add to their extraordinary knowledge or collection. The Special Interest helps to prevent meltdowns because it's calming and relaxing (discussed in detail in Chapter 14).

AVOID SITUATIONS THAT ARE STRESSFUL FOR THE ASPIE

If you're in the early days of a relationship with your Aspie, observe which activities or social situations they find distressing. Weddings, parties, family gatherings or shops are possible examples. The Aspie's frustration and anxiety levels quickly multiply with the slightest amount of stress, particularly of a social and emotional nature.

Tip: Make a mental note to avoid situations that the Aspie finds stressful, if possible. Sometimes, attending social gatherings on your own can be more enjoyable.

REMOVE THE STRESSOR

Stressors can be work commitments such as deadlines, or relationship conflicts such as an argument with your teenager. Aspies may experience added stressors from sensory issues such as barking dogs, loud music or strong odours. Talk to your Aspie about the stressors that bother them and if possible remove or decrease their intensity. If you're unable to remove the stressor it's important to comfort and support your partner.

Meltdowns and how to cope
Take a step back

Observe, rather than criticize. When a meltdown occurs, watch your partner and try to work out the triggers of their frustration and how they deal with stress. Also, take note of and encourage the methods that relax them. Avoid taking their raised voice and frustration personally. For most of the time, you won't be the cause. A more likely reason is a build-up of stress throughout the day or something out of the blue that may never be understood. When a meltdown occurs, instead of retaliating, try to empathize with your partner. Before or during the meltdown, ask yourself the questions below to increase your awareness of possible meltdown triggers:

- What do I see, hear and sense?

- Is my Aspie's frustration due to something I've done wrong? If so, apologize.

- Is their face showing signs of frustration or confusion?

- Are they speaking loudly to themselves or other people about dropping things or forgetting things?

- Are they criticizing what someone else does?

Methods for managing meltdowns

Multiple strategies can be used to decrease meltdowns. Remember, quick recovery time involves staying calm, refusing to listen to blunt words and walking away. When AS is first discovered it may be particularly difficult to do this, but with time, knowledge and experience, it becomes easier. Walking away enables you to recover quickly and move on. However on some days, this won't be possible.

Depending on the situation, sometimes it's important to intercept when your Aspie is in orange or red zone but this must be done with care. Some ways to do this are encouraging your partner to have a rest or do something relaxing, such as going for a walk or enjoying their Special Interest. Be organized by establishing a plan for those days when the 'worst case' scenarios unfold. If you prepare for red zone every day, the times when your partner is in green and orange zone are bonuses.

During a meltdown

1. Avoid communicating with the Aspie. They're unable to process information when in red zone. The worst thing you can do, which comes naturally, is to ask, 'What's wrong?' Or 'What are you angry about?' Asking questions may inflame the situation rather than help it.

2. Be one step ahead at all times. Remove self, children and pets from the person having a meltdown. Be prepared to activate Plan B if your Aspie becomes frustrated. This may involve going out with your children or friends.

3. Use statements like, 'That's unacceptable behaviour' or 'I can see you're frustrated.' Is it worth an argument and a meltdown? Walking away is easier and may be more conducive to a peaceful outcome.

4. Don't retaliate. If you engage in the fight, you give them the power and control and you're setting yourself up for failure. If you *do not* engage in the fight, *you* keep the power (your energy). By changing *your* behaviour and response, the Aspie is far more likely to look at the situation differently. Your partner may not see your point of view but it's possible they may look at their own behaviour and their part in the argument. When the Aspie is relaxed, try discussing ways to decrease or avoid conflict next time.

5. Respond calmly, rather than react. How you respond to an Aspie has a huge effect on the resolution of conflict. In the *Bible*, it says in Proverbs 15:1, 'A gentle answer turns away wrath, but a harsh word stirs up anger.' Think about what has been said or done and work out what you can say or do in response. If you speak calmly, it's more likely that the other person will reply calmly. Sometimes, silence is useful. Take a moment to reflect on conflicts you've had with your partner. How did you respond? What could you do differently next time?

Meltdown recovery

Wait until the Aspie has calmed down before you discuss the issue. This can take from five minutes to two hours or more. Sometimes it's best not to discuss the topic at all. What can you do?

- If it's trivial, let it go.

- Journalling is therapeutic as it helps to release anger and frustration, process thoughts, reflect on events and devise possible solutions for future reference (see Chapter 10).

- Spend time alone. Resting or sleeping is vital.

- It may take a few days to recover from an Aspie's major meltdown because constant insults leave you feeling exhausted.

- The highest priority is to maintain your emotional energy (see Chapter 3).

- Do something relaxing or go out with friends, because it's most likely that the Aspie will require space anyway.

IN THE ZONE: GREEN ZONE IS WHERE THE ASPIE IS RELAXED

Activities, behaviours and strategies are not necessarily related across columns.

ASPIE'S ACTIVITIES	ASPIE'S BEHAVIOUR	STRATEGIES FOR THE NT
• Watching TV and DVDs • Eating (especially junk food) • Enjoying Special Interest • Creating and building things • Appreciating nature and waterfalls	• Relaxed and quiet • Smiling or laughing • Facial expressions are relaxed	• Encourage Aspie's routine and try to keep the environment stable • Give Aspie space • Encourage Aspie to do their Special Interest • Talk about important and sensitive issues when Aspie is in green zone • Give plenty of warning and explain what is expected prior to a social activity

IN THE ZONE: ORANGE ZONE –
WARNING SIGNS OF IMPENDING MELTDOWN

Triggers, indicators and strategies are not necessarily related across columns.

TRIGGERS	ASPIE'S BEHAVIOURS AND INDICATORS	STRATEGIES FOR THE NT
SENSORY OVERLOAD ISSUES: • Too much to process at once • Become particularly stressed if tired, sick, in pain, hot, cold or hungry • Interruption to routine ASPIES FIND DEALING WITH PEOPLE STRESSFUL BECAUSE THEY: • Don't know what the other person's needs and wants are • Are 'mind-blind' (see Chapter 7 and Chapter 14) • Miss some social cues • Find others demanding and emotionally intense • Have difficulty conversing with someone while simultaneously reading their non-verbals • Feel pressured to make a decision that they may not agree with or believe in	BEHAVIOURS: • Raise voice a little or swear, especially when frustrated • Become flustered and go from one activity to another • Become frustrated when they are forgetful, drop things or lose items • Restless and agitated INDICATORS: • Difficulty concentrating • Decreased intimacy • Become hypersensitive • Red face and a facial rash • Blank look on face	COMMUNICATION: • Allow silence, avoid talking • Encourage space/solitude • Don't complain or be demanding • Listen attentively to the Aspie's concerns • Encourage them to go for a walk or engage in their Special Interest PRACTICAL IDEAS: • Limit the number of social activities • Suggest the Aspie have a sleep • Give a firm back massage or light back tickle • Distract from the source of stress • Encourage them to follow their routine • Try to maintain a stable environmental routine (see Chapter 10)

IN THE ZONE: RED ZONE IS DANGER ZONE (DON'T APPROACH)

Triggers, indicators and strategies are not necessarily related across columns.

TRIGGERS	ASPIE'S BEHAVIOURS AND INDICATORS	STRATEGIES FOR THE NT
• Triggers from the orange zone are not resolved	BEHAVIOURS: • Voice becomes very loud • Says blunt and harsh words • Has difficulty controlling their behaviour • Walks around in circles or paces • Becomes extremely agitated INDICATORS: • Phases out (withdraws) or explodes (has a meltdown) • May have a scowl on their face	COMMUNICATION: • Avoid questioning or reasoning • Never interrupt • Stay calm and speak quietly • Don't argue • Avoid trying to cheer them up PRACTICAL IDEAS: • Give space • Take the phone off the hook • Cancel planned activities • Avoid showing affection and becoming emotional

Zoning in

Some Aspies can tell you what zone they're in. This alerts you to decrease stress around them if possible. The challenge for you is deciding which zone they're in: green, orange or red.

The reference used for information on meltdowns in this chapter is from Minds and Hearts Clinic: A Specialist Clinic for Autism and Asperger's Syndrome. The clinic is in West End, Brisbane, Australia. Their internet site is www.mindsandhearts.net.

Take away tips

- You can't fix meltdowns but you can control *how you respond*.
- Try not to overload yourself with a busy schedule.
- Be one step ahead of the Aspie at all times.
- Try not to be stressed or emotional.
- Speak calmly and clearly.
- Don't take the Aspie's insults personally.
- Observe, rather than criticize.
- Avoid talking to the Aspie if they're irritated.
- Don't retaliate or react, it never works.
- Maintain a calm and structured environment.
- Avoid trying to resolve conflict when the Aspie is in meltdown mode.
- Solitude, space, distractions and Special Interests are important.
- During a meltdown, it's preferable not to engage with the Aspie.

Conclusion

As you negotiate the maze of intimacy, there comes a point when the arguments and meltdowns decrease. By using strategies outlined in this chapter, you'll have more energy, and over time your partner will have fewer meltdowns. Strategies may work for one couple, but not for others.

As you can see from the *In the Zone charts* many stressors and triggers can send your partner into red zone. Aspies are visual and logical people;

the way the charts are presented should strike a chord. Try showing your partner these charts when they're in green zone and discuss the triggers that set them off. Once you're aware of the stressors, you'll know what to avoid. Discover together what works for your relationship. Perhaps devising your own personal couple chart could be something to work on together.

Just Enough Light

Sometimes only the step I'm on,
Or the very next one ahead,
Is all that is illuminated for me
God gives just the amount of light I need

For the exact moment I need it.
At those times I walk in surrender to faith,
Unable to see the future
And not fully comprehending the past.

And because it is God who has given me
What light I have,
I know I must reject the fear and
Doubt that threaten to overtake me.

I must determine to be content where
I am, and allow God to get me where I
Need to go.
I walk forward,

One step at a time
Fully trusting that
The light God sheds
Is absolutely sufficient.

© Stormie Omartian (2008)

Chapter 10

Regaining Your Identity

Regaining your identity begins with letting go of preconceived ideas, giving up your dreams of the perfect relationship and working through the Grief Process. Only then can you move on, begin to develop your talents and pursue true happiness.

What *defines* you? What *legacy* do you hope to leave for future generations? Discovering your purpose and goals for the future will encourage you to pursue personal growth. Are you ready to regain your identity? Before this is even considered, the 'grief and loss process' and 'healing process' need to be worked through. While moving through the stages of grief, let go of expectations of how your Aspie should relate to you.

Let go of the dream of the 'perfect' relationship

When you're hit with the realization that your partner has AS, it's comparable to a balloon bursting. You're stunned, as all your hopes and dreams of a happy, close, intimate relationship are lost. Let go of these dreams and expectations. You can still dream, but now it's different. Let the old dreams go. As you work through the grief, things will become easier. As the saying goes, 'If you love something, set it free; if it comes back to you, it's yours – if it doesn't, it never was' (Unknown).

Reconnect with yourself

Reconnecting with yourself and redefining your identity are crucial steps in the healing process as illustrated in the following story:

I came to the realization that my husband had AS and *I* needed to change. The stark truth was that I had lost my identity. Trying to save our marriage for so long left me exhausted. I found it was vital to *reconnect with myself* totally and discover 'me' again, spiritually, emotionally and physically. I suddenly started thinking, 'Where is that person I was when I first married?' With counselling and support, life started to improve. Excitement came with finding myself again, but with that came a disturbing sense of loss and intense sorrow. Throughout the relationship, I felt that I couldn't cope emotionally. My basic self was still there, although an absence of true happiness and purpose in life was a reality. My identity had been eroded because my emotional needs were unfulfilled for a long time. I came to realize that my self-esteem is not dependent on what other people think of me but what I think of myself, and accepting myself for who I am. I don't need to perform to gain acceptance; I'm already acceptable. If I need to make some changes in my life, then I'll make those changes, and that rebuilds my self-esteem. There's no need to persecute or punish myself if I make a mistake. I don't rely on my husband's affection for my self-worth, because *I'm worth more than I can ever imagine*. I know he loves and appreciates me and I now accept that his lack of expression of this is not a reflection of who I am, or what I'm worth. (Anon 2008)

The Kübler-Ross Grief Process

Elisabeth Kübler-Ross explains the grieving process as having five stages: denial, anger, bargaining, depression and acceptance. A person can go in and out of the different stages of grief or sometimes become stuck in one stage. These are discussed further in *On Grief and Grieving* by Kübler-Ross and Kessler, and *Loss and Grief* by Gressor. This is an individual journey, so continue through the stages at your own pace. The grieving process is quite normal and can take years to work through. Causes of grief include death, divorce or *the loss of the dream* of the 'happily-ever-after' relationship. Some losses in an AS/NT relationship include loss of self-esteem, identity and the 'perfect' relationship.

Before you reach the acceptance stage of the Grief Process, it's imperative to forgive your partner to avoid resentment. To deal with this, individual and couple counselling can be extremely helpful. Try not to blame the Aspie – and don't blame yourself either. As you gain emotional strength, you'll relate more effectively to your partner. Be encouraged – with the help of your supportive network, you will come through this. Regaining your identity will be easier, once you've worked through the grief. An excellent website describing Elisabeth Kübler-Ross' work is recommended in the bibliography of this book.

The 'Eight-Stage Healing Process'

People with AS don't have a disease, rather, their brain is wired differently to that of the NT. This section outlines a continual healing process for NTs who are grieving, and wish to move on and gain hope for their relationship with their Aspie. The 'Eight-Stage Healing Process for Families and Friends of the Mentally Ill' has been adapted for those living with an Aspie from a book by Julie Tallard Johnson called *Hidden Victims, Hidden Healers*.

Stage 1: Awareness

Have you searched for years to find an answer regarding your Aspie's behaviour? Are you exhausted from the constant frustration, anxiety, anger and meltdowns? Family and friends either advise you to end the relationship or say, 'It's normal.' In the early days of the relationship, did you feel torn between wanting to stay or leave because deep down you still loved them?

You may have consulted professionals for answers, especially in relation to personal mental health issues such as anxiety and depression. Desperate, your search continues; it seems endless – until you find out about AS. The light goes on. The pieces of this puzzle all fit together in an odd sort of way.

Throughout this stage, it's helpful to make a 'personal inventory' of feelings that you experience such as fear, guilt, hostility and resentment, as described by Johnson in *Hidden Victims, Hidden Healers*. Journalling is a useful method of self-reflection that brings you back to focusing on yourself, promoting forgiveness and healing. If you've worked through the Grief Process, healing will occur more readily. Remember, you can only change yourself. Start by thinking, 'What can *I* do to change the way *I* relate and respond to my loved one?'

Stage 2: Validation

How do you feel at the moment – exhausted, guilty or angry? Talking to your family and friends about your concerns or seeking professional counselling may be helpful. When AS is first suspected, you may experience a feeling of relief that you're not going mad. It's reassuring to know that a reason exists for all the upheaval in the relationship. People who don't understand AS may try to minimize it and say meltdowns are normal, when you know they're not.

In *Hidden Victims, Hidden Healers* Julie Johnson encourages people to search their hearts to see if they have any repressed feelings like anger or resentment. It may be beneficial to share your story with others in a similar situation. Joining a support group and seeking counselling can help with this stage (see Chapter 13). Increasing your supportive network by making friends with like-minded NTs is really important. Venting helps you release the emotional pain. Avoid people who encourage negative feelings such as guilt and fear, which is a point emphasized by Julie Johnson in *Hidden Victims, Hidden Healers*. Instead of dwelling on the negatives, share your feelings with those close to you and move on to the next stage.

Stage 3: Acceptance

The first step in stage three involves giving up control. You can't control anyone's behaviour, except your own. Do you try to control everything the Aspie does? Are you a Caretaker or a Codependent (see Chapter 5)? If you let go of control, there may be a chance that the Aspie can actually start being themselves. So, take the focus off your partner, redirect it to yourself and be responsible for *your* part in the relationship. Begin working on yourself and ask, 'What can *I* do to improve the dynamics of the relationship?'

The second step to reaching acceptance is looking after your emotional well-being (see Chapter 3). What small things can you do to keep your sanity for one more day? Perhaps a walk along the beach or enjoying nature will refresh you? Adequate sleep and rest are extremely important in replenishing energy so that you can deal with the Aspie's meltdowns. Try to meet your own needs, seek personal counselling if required and enjoy your supportive network.

Stage 4: Challenge

In *Hidden Victims, Hidden Healers*, Julie Johnson explains that this stage is where expectations and beliefs are identified and examined. Are you continually worried that you don't live up to your partner's expectations? Do you have overly high expectations of yourself? If so, is it possible for you to acknowledge, review and lower those expectations? If you always live up to other people's expectations, perhaps it's time to write your *own* life rules. When you 'let go of' expectations of yourself and those of your partner, peace and freedom will follow.

GIVE YOURSELF PERMISSION TO HAVE AN 'IMPERFECT' RELATIONSHIP

The reality is that no relationship is perfect. Trying to maintain a façade of being perfect only drains your energy, promotes a sense of failure and increases resentment. The fact is that every relationship has its challenges. Set your partner and yourself free from being the perfect couple in the perfect relationship.

One wife married to an Aspie commented:

> The words, 'Give yourself permission to have an "imperfect" relationship' are very powerful and let you off the hook. They have really touched me because I always felt I had perfect parents, a perfect upbringing and perfect children. However, my marriage was anything but perfect. (Anon 2009)

Stage 5: Releasing guilt

A beginning step is admitting your part in the relationship breakdown. Holding on to guilt may result in bitterness and resentment which will take a toll on your emotional and physical health. It's necessary to relinquish these feelings so that you can move through the healing process. Remember not to blame the Aspie or yourself for the things that have happened. Blaming doesn't solve anything; it just makes things worse. Rather than focusing on the little things, which may seem huge, it's helpful to try to see the bigger picture. Try and move on from past issues and accept your partner as they are. You can't change the past so it's important to let it go, move on and enjoy your future.

Stage 6: Forgiveness

Resentment creates a wedge in relationships. Forgiveness dislodges the wedge as you shift from one 'type' of dream and create a different dream based on your newly gained knowledge of AS. This dream brings a fresh perspective and beginning. Once you change your perspective, the issues causing the resentment aren't the same. You're in the *same* relationship; you just need to view it from a *different* angle. As the resentment is dealt with, it's really important to allow yourself to work through each stage of the healing process.

FORGIVE YOURSELF AND YOUR PARTNER

While forgiving is very powerful and freeing, unforgiveness leads to bitterness as well as adversely affecting your health. If a person harbours bitterness, their heart rate and blood pressure can increase, possibly being linked to coronary artery disease and even premature death; a point made by Carlson, Martin and Buskist in their book *Psychology*. Ultimately, if you feel hostility, blame and anger, it's imperative that you forgive yourself and your partner.

It may be hard to forgive your Aspie, especially if you've been constantly rejected. Often, they don't know they've hurt you. Life is far too valuable to spend time being resentful and angry towards your partner. Avoid deliberately paying back your Aspie by hurting them.

Forgiveness is not a feeling, but a decision – a very freeing decision. Instead of being stuck in the 'pay-back' cycle, release negative thoughts about yourself and your Aspie. Try replacing these thoughts with positive ones by focusing your energy on more worthwhile and productive things, such as establishing a new hobby or doing something special for yourself, as Julie Johnson suggests in her book *Hidden Victims, Hidden Healers*.

Finally, don't be too hard on yourself. Be patient, as it may take some time for healing to occur and for you to 'turn over a new leaf'.

Stage 7: Self-esteem

Self-worth is extremely important. If you've been badly hurt by blunt and harsh words, it's likely that you will have low self-esteem. This stage is about appreciating and honouring yourself for the person you are. One way to do this is through positive affirmations. Change negative thoughts about yourself into positive ones. An example is, if your Aspie says, 'You're stupid,' change it to a positive statement like, 'Actually, I'm a very intelligent person.' Repeat the affirmations regularly throughout the day, for a few weeks or as long as required. You could also express yourself through journalling or writing a poem.

Loneliness may lead to low self-esteem. Have you become a 'social and emotional widow'? This means that your partner hasn't died but social and emotional fulfilment is absent, leaving you feeling incomplete. Take some of the focus off your partner and redirect it to yourself. As mentioned frequently in this book, it's important to maintain your energy. This can be achieved by looking after yourself, while still being there for the Aspie. With increased self-esteem, personal growth can occur.

Stage 8: Growth

Give yourself praise and acknowledgement for the accomplishments that you've achieved. Now is the ideal time to think about *your* purpose and find out who you *really* are. Although this is the last stage of the healing process, it's a significant step to moving on with your life and regaining your identity.

Regaining your identity

How would you describe yourself? Take a few moments to write a list of your qualities, for example, good listener, honest, patient, caring and empathic.

Where are you going?

You need to know *where* you're going. Write down some goals that are achievable, measurable and can be completed in a realistic time-frame. Include daily, weekly, monthly, short-term, medium (two years) and long-term (five years) goals. Start with small goals like sitting in the sun or enjoying a relaxing bubble bath once a week. Reviewing goals on a regular basis reminds you where you're going and what you've accomplished.

What to take on the journey

When you go on a hiking trip, you might take food, water, maps, a compass and a watch. A personal growth journey requires motivation, goals, direction, discipline, healthy boundaries and the ability to look after yourself. Writing in a journal may be helpful to define goals, describe the journey and reflect on your progress. Often when you go through difficult times, it can be hard to see the positives, especially when the journey seems long. Like the hiker, you need a compass and a map. The compass symbolizes the goals that lead you in the right direction. The map, or journal, is to remind you not only of where you're going, but where you've come from and the obstacles you've overcome.

Find out who you really are

The beginning steps in this process are accepting yourself and improving your self-esteem. Knowing who you are and what you believe in is crucial to discovering your purpose. Think about what you would like to achieve in *your* life. God has a plan for your life. In the *Bible*, Jeremiah 29:11 states, 'For I know the plans I have for you', declares the Lord, 'plans to prosper you and not to harm you, plans to give you hope and a future.' If your creator has a plan and purpose for you, it's important that you do too.

Childhood dreams

What did you enjoy doing when you were a child or a teenager? Did you have a talent that you discontinued, for example, dancing, singing, sport or painting? Do you ever wish you could develop this talent again? Be encouraged, you *can* do what you set out to do. No one is stopping you, except yourself.

The road to regaining your identity

When the journey begins, you may be exhausted. This results in withdrawing and being less available to love your partner, due to rebuilding your life. Even though desperate for love and belonging, you may have very little love to give your partner whilst working through the Grief Process. You can only give out of the resources you have. When love levels are low, you won't be able to give as much to others. Regaining your life and boosting your emotional energy are *crucial* in bringing new life to your relationship.

Build a protective wall around you

As you regain your identity, visualize a protective wall around you – like a shield that repels all the negative criticism. Once you're happy and content with your life, negative remarks will be repelled, instead of being taken to heart. The next stage of the journey involves examining your hierarchy of needs and how these needs can be fulfilled.

Maslow's 'Hierarchy of Needs'

The motivational theory model of the late psychologist, Abraham Maslow, consists of five stages, and is explained by Baden Eunson in his book *Communicating in the 21st Century*. These stages are discussed, incorporating a comparison of the NTs and the Aspie's needs. By progressing through the stages of the hierarchy, a person is able to work on developing their self-esteem and reaching their full potential.

Refer to Maslow's 'Hierarchy of Needs' (p.133). Read from the broad base at the bottom of the triangle, where the most vital and basic needs are, working upwards towards the pinnacle, where self-actualization is realized.

Maslow's 'Hierarchy of Needs'

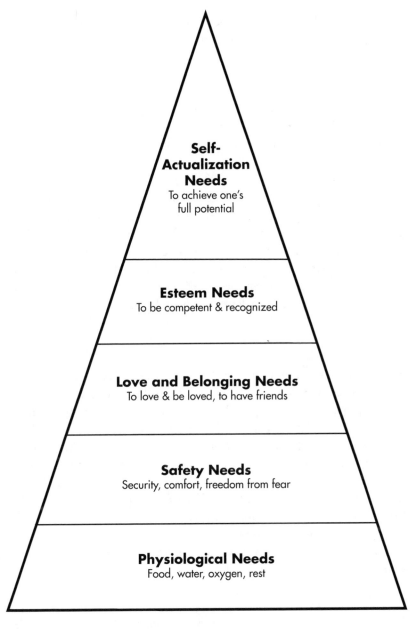

**Self-
Actualization
Needs**
To achieve one's
full potential

Esteem Needs
To be competent & recognized

Love and Belonging Needs
To love & be loved, to have friends

Safety Needs
Security, comfort, freedom from fear

Physiological Needs
Food, water, oxygen, rest

Adapted from p.605 of Carlson, Martin and Buskist (2004)

The NT's needs

Safety needs

We all need to feel emotionally and physically safe. Harsh words from the Aspie can lead to the NT's emotional and physical safety being compromised. Once you put strategies from Chapters 8 and 9 into place, you'll be able to deal more effectively with the Aspie's blunt and harsh words, making it easier to feel close to them. Develop a supportive network of family or friends to meet your safety needs if a crisis occurs. If you're neglected emotionally in an AS/NT relationship, it would be reasonable to suggest that your love and belonging needs haven't been met.

Love and belonging

Often, NTs experience a deep sense of satisfaction through comforting, encouraging or inspiring others, whilst neglecting their own desperate need to *receive* love. Unfortunately, the Aspie may be unaware of how to fulfil your love and belonging needs. It's important to guide them and explain literally what your needs are and how they can meet them. Another way for you to meet these needs is to pursue fulfilment in other healthy relationships. Insufficient love and belonging can lead to low self-esteem.

Self-esteem

As Baden Eunson points out in his book, *Communicating in the 21st Century*, Maslow talks about high self-esteem being vital as it assists in achieving goals, status, responsibility and reputation. Through years of verbal abuse, belittling and heartache from being misunderstood, it's likely that your self-esteem has been ripped to shreds. Consequently, there may be a lack of energy or motivation to reach self-actualization.

As self-esteem improves, you'll feel better about yourself and know that you're valuable and significant. You'll be happier, healthier and feel free to move on. The need for constant approval and affection from the Aspie will be reduced because you now feel comfortable with yourself and who you are. The fact is: *the Aspie's lack of affection does not reflect on your value or who you are.*

Self-actualization

In *Communicating in the 21st Century*, on p.383, Baden Eunson explains how Maslow suggests that if you have completed the 'lower hierarchy of needs', you may be able to attain self-actualization which is the need to 'be all that one can be, the need to achieve one's ultimate human potential'. As a consequence of being in a relationship with an Aspie, self-actualization may not have been attained. If you achieved it prior to this relationship, you could have lost it and need to regain it. When beginning the journey to self-actualization, care about yourself *first*. Once you've regained your identity, regardless of reaching self-actualization, you'll be able to withstand most hardships in the AS/NT relationship.

The Aspie's Needs
Safety needs
Everyone has a basic requirement to feel that the world is predictable, organized and stable. Safety needs are met through feeling secure, emotionally and physically.

Listen to two Aspies' perspectives:

STORY A

> I feel safe when things are predictable and stable. I like relationships where the other person is consistent and stable. (Anon 2008)

STORY B

> My *environmental routine* needs to be stable at all times for me to stay in green zone. If you encourage me to do my Special Interest when my environmental routine is not *exactly* the same as it normally is, I can easily go into orange or red zone. Irritations and meltdowns could happen frequently if a change in my routine or my family's routine occurs.
>
> Environmental routine means everyone and everything in the family and household has to stay the same. If the household routine becomes disrupted, it really upsets me. An example is when my wife was on leave from work, she wasn't using the bathroom at exactly the same time as usual. This disrupted the order of *my* routine.
>
> Television shows have to be on at exactly the same time. I become really annoyed when my favourite show is moved to a different time because sport has replaced it. Watching that programme is part of my routine that I enjoy immensely.
>
> My rigid routine makes me feel happy, safe, on familiar ground and secure. Everything needs to be in its right place and working well. Family

> members need to be consistent in what they do. *Environmental routine is equally as important as enjoying and concentrating on my Special Interest.* (Anon 2009)

Isn't it reasonable to deduce from these statements that Aspies may not always have their safety needs met due to the many, unpredictable situations in everyday life? This must be extremely stressful for them.

Even sensory issues that you take for granted are difficult for your partner. Some Aspies are perpetually worried and harassed due to life's unpredictability. Just coping with everyday issues is a challenge for them. They have a lot of difficulty feeling comfortable in their environment. It needs to be organized and controlled, for example, the temperature has to be perfect and their personal items may have to be arranged in a certain way. For these reasons, it's helpful if you can empathize with your partner and what they are going through.

If an Aspie finds it difficult to be at peace, is it any wonder they don't feel safe? If their level of anxiety decreases, they might move on to the next level, which is love and belonging. They can regress at any time and move between the levels in Maslow's 'Hierarchy of Needs'. If the Aspie doesn't feel emotionally safe, they may have difficulty expressing and feeling comfortable with love and belonging.

Love and belonging

Many Aspies have felt estranged at times, especially during childhood, as a result of rejection, criticism and bullying. Self-protection against alienation becomes a daily goal, as does fitting in and making friends.

How do Aspies fulfil their love and belonging needs, when most have few, if any, friends? Struggling with relationship difficulties may lead to further insecurities and a possible absence of love and belonging. In *Communicating in the 21st Century*, Eunson describes love and belonging needs as social needs, requiring the company of other people.

A basic human instinct is to feel that you belong and are accepted by a family or a group of people who share common goals or ideas. The fact is that we all need to feel connected to others. Even though many Aspies enjoy spending lengthy periods of time alone, it doesn't mean that they don't have any love and belonging needs. Actually, quite the opposite is true. Listen to one female Aspie's view:

> For Aspies, belonging and feeling accepted is as important (if not more important) than it is for NTs. Also, love is a necessity for many Aspies. We just have a slightly different take on what it might look like. (Anon 2009)

Self-esteem

The next level, of esteem and status, is unattainable if the Aspie hasn't fulfilled their 'love and belonging' needs. Feelings of loneliness can lead to anxiety and depression. If anxiety and depression continue, suggest they seek help from their doctor. Through encouraging the development of your partner's positive attributes and involvement in the Special Interest, their self-esteem is likely to increase.

NTs should be careful not to judge Aspies. One Aspie said, 'I'll never be good enough. I never get it right' (Anon 2009). Aspies can't be expected to progress through the stages of Maslow's 'Hierarchy of Needs' if they're being discouraged at each level. It's akin to climbing a ladder and being constantly pulled down to the rung below each time you start to climb. Frustration ensues as the Aspie believes they will never make it to the top, to reach self-actualization. They still have a need to belong and *feel worthwhile*. This can be achieved by the NT giving the Aspie frequent praise when it is due and encouraging their Special Interest.

Self-actualization

The Aspie achieves self-actualization through engaging in their Special Interest which makes them feel emotionally safe. If love and belonging and self-esteem needs haven't been met, your partner may not be able to fully reach self-actualization. Is it any wonder they want to engage frequently in their Special Interest? This makes them feel extremely happy and at peace.

SPECIAL INTEREST STORIES

A female Aspie shared her story:

> For the Aspie, a sense of self is very often derived from the relationship with their *special interest*. Most humans derive a sense of self from their relationships with others, as well as other factors, such as career, hobbies, etc. For us, the focus can be a little more singular and systematic. If the Aspie is allowed to derive their sense of self from their *special interest*, they can achieve some happiness and fulfilment in a world that makes little or even no sense to them. It's helpful if the NT partner tries to understand

that the Aspie needs the *special interest*, like any human needs to breathe. If this can be factored in and understood within the parameters of the relationship, it can be enriching for all involved.

The AS/NT relationship is certainly different to the norm. However, it can be wonderful and exciting, all the same. Most often, the key to a meaningful life is inextricably linked in with my *special interest*. I bond with my painting, as I express myself most fully, through it. In actual fact, the *special interest* allows me the expression of emotional range and subtlety – the very things we often can't achieve in relationships with other people 'in the moment'. The *special interest* is where the fullest manifestation of self can be actualized and experienced. Most certainly in my case, best outcomes in terms of quality of life can be achieved when I'm encouraged to develop my interest as my vocation and career. The *special interest* fuses with me. It allows for a complete and relaxed sense of who I am. (Anon 2009)

A male Aspie shared:

Self-actualization is achieved through my Special Interest. As well as feeling inspired, a deep sense of personal satisfaction, achievement and self-worth is experienced through my Special Interest. I feel emotionally safe when doing my project, because I'm in my comfort zone. (Anon 2009)

Take away tips

- What *defines* you?
- What *legacy* do you hope to leave for the next generation?
- View your relationship from a different angle.
- Let go of the dream of the 'perfect' relationship.
- Deal with your grief.
- Forgiving others helps you to move on.
- Find out who you *really* are.
- Remember the importance of personal growth and increasing your self-esteem.
- The Special Interest is crucial to the Aspie's happiness, so respect it.

- What are *your* needs?

- How can you regain your identity?

Conclusion

Instead of repeatedly vying for your partner's attention, *choose to make a life for yourself.* Pursuing your interests will bring great happiness. Regaining your identity is one of the *most important journeys* in personal growth that you'll ever make. Remember, 'Let go of your expectations' and work through the grief. Once you find yourself again, your self-esteem will start to improve. *Don't give up; hope can be found.*

If you pursue your purpose and regain your identity, your partner is more likely to draw emotionally closer. Although AS symptoms such as sensory overload, frustration and anxiety will always be there, AS/NT relationships can improve. Once the goal of regaining your identity has been achieved, you're ready to commence attempts to reconnect with your partner. This will be discussed in the next chapter.

Chapter 11

Beginning to Reconnect

'Ask yourself why you chose this relationship in the first instance and then choose to recommit.' (Anon NT, married to an Aspie for 48 years)

Take a few minutes to imagine the moment you first caught your partner's eye. Think of the place, fragrances, noises, what you were both wearing and the topic of discussion. Can you remember the cherished emotional or physical closeness, the 'butterflies' as the world stood still? Perhaps you wish you could freeze this instant forever.

At the beginning of your relationship it's likely that *you* were the Special Interest. Over time, or even after the honeymoon, your partner may not have treated you as the special project any more. Generally, it's not intentional that Aspies neglect you or isolate themselves. They simply pursue their Special Interest because it provides them with purpose, energy and pleasure.

One Aspie shared:

> To the Aspie, the special project (to find a wife) is over; it's been achieved. Now he moves on to the next project. The Aspie still loves his wife but may be unaware of what to do to maintain the relationship. This apathy can look like they don't make any effort, when it's likely they may be trying really hard to connect with the NT. (Anon 2007)

You may never be the Special Interest again. However, this chapter provides helpful hints on how to reconnect with your partner. Before you read further, write down some ways that you and your partner can reconnect. Do something pleasant such as taking a walk, enjoying a break at a café or cooking together or for each other.

Clueless about romance?

You need someone to understand you, provide comfort and share happy or sad moments. The Aspie wants to connect but may not know how. They may be clueless as to what's expected in a romantic relationship, as well as how to behave socially. Help them to understand, instead of complaining that they never care or comprehend what you're going through. Tell them what your needs are and how they can best meet those needs.

Where to begin?

Reconnecting can be both exciting and scary. Currently, you may be experiencing feelings of doubt, guilt, uncertainty and vulnerability, as well as the fear of being hurt. It takes great courage to reconnect. It may be helpful to give your partner many new ideas about how to relate to you on a daily basis.

Let go of the past

If pain keeps you in the past, it may be difficult to move on with your life. Decide that *you* will take responsibility for moving forward. Personal and marital counselling is extremely beneficial in helping to deal with unresolved past and current issues. If possible, deal with feelings of guilt and hurt by forgiving quickly and often.

Regaining your identity enhances reconnecting

As mentioned in the previous chapter, the secret is to reconnect with yourself, prior to reconnecting with your partner. Your self-confidence will slowly rebuild through participating in enjoyable and rejuvenating activities, accepting and loving yourself, and refusing to accept abuse. Subsequently, when you feel more content with who you are, letting go becomes easier and reconnecting more appealing. The need to compete with your partner decreases and the likelihood of both partners desiring intimacy increases.

Allow your partner to be a unique individual

As you're regaining your identity, encourage your loved one to do the same. It's really important to allow your partner to be themselves with their own beliefs and dreams. Regular encouragement with regards to their Special Interest is vital.

Introduce changes slowly

Most Aspies will have difficulty with the changes you instigate concerning your identity. They prefer to have a structured routine and a stable partner who remains the same forever. If you plan to try something new – introduce small changes, one at a time. Warn them before changing your hairstyle or regularly attending social activities for the first time in years.

These personal changes are positive and vital, leading to increased self-esteem. With time and persistence, you'll become happy, independent and self-sufficient again. If you're happy and independent, it's more likely your partner will move closer to you. Aspies actually prefer to be with someone who is organized and independent, as this reduces stress.

Attentive listening deepens the connection

Through attentive listening, you can draw emotionally closer to your partner (review Chapter 6). In *The Dance of Connection*, Harriet Lerner suggests that if this is done in a caring manner, there may be a deepening of the connection between two people.

Change the way you relate to your partner

It takes time to learn new ways of relating. You may react to your Aspie because you're stuck in the old ways of reacting to each other. Give up the old way in your head and say, 'Today is a new day and we're starting out a new way.' Sometimes, when you're implementing techniques from a counselling session or a book you've read, the old ways might creep in. You may still have the 'old tapes' playing. Stop the old tapes and make new ones together.

Successfully compliment your partner

One male Aspie explained:

> When you give praise to your partner, give them a 100 per cent compliment, not a 0 per cent compliment. You have to prove to the Aspie that you want to be on their page emotionally. Remember, everything is black or white to the Aspie (you either give a compliment or you don't). An example of a 0 per cent compliment is, 'Oh, that's very nice, Honey.' You think you've given a 100 per cent compliment, when it's actually been interpreted as a 0 per cent compliment (the Aspie has received *nothing* from this comment).

On the other hand, a 100 per cent compliment might consist of an intelligent question coupled with praise, like, 'Wow! That looks like a good plan for your electronic project. What items do you need to make it work?' This will successfully boost his self-esteem. (Anon 2009)

Guidelines for reconnecting

Do you think you and your partner are heading in the same direction? Are you both willing to make an effort in a bid to be happy and improve your relationship? Listed below are some important tips. Perhaps you could add more?

- Both partners need to deal with unresolved past issues.
- Individual and marital counselling is imperative and can be life changing.
- Be companions first.
- Don't criticize or judge your partner.
- Ensure work and leisure time is balanced.
- Expect less of each other. Remember, if you don't have any expectations, you won't have any disappointments.
- Being physically and emotionally relaxed around your partner is important.
- Adopt appropriate healthy boundaries.
- It's ideal if both partners are motivated and really want the relationship to improve.
- Enjoy reconnecting activities when both partners are well, energetic and are keen to be involved.
- Appreciate the close, happy moments, especially if they happen rarely.

Strategies to reconnect
Let them off the hook by backing off
One NT partner shared:

> One Friday, my husband agreed to drive me to the partners' support group the next morning. He would spend the day enjoying his Special Interest, while I went to the meeting. The next morning, I found him lying on the bed

with the pillow over his head, which meant he was in red zone. Sensing he was stressed, I said, 'Love, I don't want you to be held up in traffic, I can drive myself to the meeting, you go and have a lovely day doing your Special Interest.' He replied, 'Really?' His face showed relief that I had let him off the hook. (Anon 2008)

Backing off relieved the Aspie by taking the pressure off him, when he was already stressed. Subsequently, a meltdown was avoided. If you're genuinely nice to an Aspie, they may reciprocate in a pleasant manner. As a result, they may slowly draw closer to you.

Comments from the NT in the above story:

This was a real turn around for our relationship. Self-control on the NTs part is vital. It has taken enormous courage for me to change and avoid retaliating, but it's worth the effort. I can let go because I feel content with who I am, now that I'm my old self again. (Anon 2008)

Seek personal and marital counselling

One NT woman shared:

I was very cautious about reconnecting with my husband because I was afraid of being emotionally hurt. I was psychologically exhausted and physically sick. It was difficult to find my real self due to the loss of my identity. It seemed like I had become someone else in order to cope with the marriage. Upset and cranky, I found it hard to love my partner; I had almost given up trying. The pain in my heart was very intense as I realized my behaviour was deteriorating. It dawned on me that I had lost my identity. This shocking realization caused me to seek personal and marital counselling. (Anon 2008)

Humour

Try tuning in to the quirky or funny side of your partner. Have you forgotten how to have a good belly laugh? Laughter and happiness are essential ingredients needed for you to feel good about yourself. It's common knowledge that Aspies are generally serious people, so 'lightening up' is the medicine they need. Humour doesn't occur very often in a troubled relationship. When the Aspie is humourous, make the most of it. If you play along with the joke, they might too. The Aspie's quirky, almost childlike sense of humour relieves tension and may defuse stressful situations.

One NT wife shared her reconnecting story:

Since I've backed off and started to read more about AS, I look at life differently. My husband and I are starting to have moments where we actually connect, which we haven't done for a long time. At some level, our sense of humour works with each other. The other day he told a funny story, I got it and just followed on with it and the joke continued. Our adult daughter thought we were acting like a couple of kids. At the moment of the joke we laughed, looked into each other's eyes and connected; it was just lovely. It's so important to enjoy and build on humorous times when they occur. (Anon 2008)

Be genuinely interested in your partner's world

Some Aspies have low self-esteem and don't even realize this. It's therefore important to give encouragement and reassurance to your partner every day. Start with the little things like, 'You're doing a fantastic job with the garden.' Ask them about their Special Interest, hobbies, work and thoughts about life. When you start to win their confidence, they may start to open up.

Reconnect through the Aspie's Special Interest

Think of interesting, smart and appropriate questions to ask with regards to their Special Interest.

An Aspie shared:

Ask an intelligent question in relation to what he is talking about or showing you. This will make him feel important and boost his self-esteem. NTs are always trying to make the Aspie see what's socially acceptable. How about being on his page by becoming intellectually appealing? You'll find after a few months of listening to him ramble on about his favourite topic, you'll become quite knowledgeable about it. This is one way of becoming closer. (Anon 2008)

Try novel ways of surprising your partner

Put a chocolate on their pillow, make a treasure hunt or write a romantic note.

Do fun things together

Be spontaneous; create and treasure memories. Take photos so that you can spend time reminiscing together in the future.

Enjoy common interests

Discuss what you have in common with your partner and what you both enjoy. Make plans for holidays and days out. Build up these activities so they become a regular part of the routine.

Learn new activities together

Attempt rock climbing, cycling, canoeing, scrap booking, ten-pin bowling, etc.

Teamwork can sometimes draw a couple together

- Use your joint talents to help someone in need or assist a charity or community.

- Work on a project or goal together: plant a garden or make plans for retirement.

Offer genuine praise and express gratitude

Aspies thrive on praise. If they're in orange zone, find some way to encourage their efforts. Praise increases their self-esteem and calms them. Thank them for any little thing they do for you. What can you say to your partner to thank and praise them?

Plan emotionally intimate times together

Connecting emotionally can be difficult, although not impossible, in an AS/NT relationship. Where did you meet? What attracted you to your partner? Try some of the following to rekindle the spark:

- Revisit special places of first dates like parks, restaurants, etc.

- Take turns deciding where to go or what to do.

- Alternate talking about things that matter to you, while your partner listens and vice versa.

- Avoid talking about stressful subjects which could lead to conflict.

- Find new topics to discuss.

- Have fun, be silly and hold hands.

- Aspies may feel pressured when asked to talk, so instead of 'talking', interact through playing cards or a board game.

Join a support group

Partners in these groups may share personal, reconnecting strategies that work in their relationships. Somehow, when you know you're not the only one in a situation, you feel empowered and motivated to try to reconnect.

Take away tips

- Seek personal and marital counselling.
- Use humour.
- Do fun things together.
- Enjoy common interests.
- Rekindle the memories.
- Change the way you relate to your partner.
- Reconnect through the Aspie's Special Interest.
- Take the pressure off the Aspie by backing off.
- As your self-esteem increases, generously praise and encourage your partner.

Conclusion

Attempting to reconnect with your Aspie might be difficult if you've forgotten how to be close and share your deepest thoughts with them. This chapter has provided guidelines for reconnecting and numerous ideas to assist you. If you make an effort to spend quality time together and be involved in mutually satisfying, reconnecting activities, there will be an improvement in your relationship. Work on building loving moments with your partner. In the next chapter, you will learn how to connect intimately with your loved one.

Chapter 12

Connecting Intimately

'I want to experience some sort of connection, some sort of normality that I've noticed in others.' (Anon Aspie 2009)

Connecting intimately is unique to the human race. According to Maslow's 'Hierarchy of Needs', to connect intimately one must feel physically and emotionally safe (see Chapter 10). Do you desperately need to be understood and long for affection, closeness and quality time? This chapter explores the issues surrounding emotional and sexual intimacy, offering strategies to help you and your partner feel emotionally safe.

Emotional and physical safety

If a person doesn't feel safe, it's unlikely that they will desire intimacy of any kind. An environment free from verbal, physical, emotional and sexual abuse is imperative. With regards to emotional safety, Aspies feel safe when their 'comforting routines' are maintained or encouraged, while most NTs experience emotional safety when quality time is shared with their partner. One Aspie shared his thoughts: 'The NT wants to *emotionally connect* with the Aspie, whereas the Aspie needs to *feel emotionally safe* before they connect' (Anon Aspie 2009).

Methods to help your partner feel emotionally safe:

- Avoid anger, bullying, intimidation, mocking and contempt. These behaviours destroy emotional safety as partners are unable to move towards each other or feel secure enough to make themselves emotionally vulnerable.

- Encourage the Special Interest or passion.

- Be involved with your own life, instead of being caught up in the Aspie's life.

- Ask some intelligent questions when involved in a technical conversation.
- Be reassuring and empathic.
- Understand that the Aspie has limited social or emotional intuition, so it's important to assist them lovingly in this area.

Tip: If you want an emotional connection, you need to help your partner feel emotionally safe.

Emotional intimacy

What comes to your mind when you think of emotional intimacy? Twenty NTs were interviewed regarding their understanding of what constitutes emotional intimacy. Both genders were represented equally in the survey. Some of their anonymous comments were:

- connecting, being 'on the same page'
- knowing that your partner is there for you, no matter what
- feeling emotionally safe and comfortable with each other
- being conscious of the other person's feelings and needs, as well as encouraging them to follow their dreams
- respecting your partner's emotions
- working together, encouraging and supporting each other
- being able to sit together and enjoy the silence
- sharing frankly your deepest, emotional and intimate thoughts, including desires, ambitions and secrets
- problem solving together
- enjoying the same interests
- unbridled, mutual self-disclosure, the act of offering oneself to another in return for acceptance, respect, compassion and support.

After reading the above points, what conclusions have you drawn? Do you have this intimacy with your partner? If you have, congratulations! If you haven't, you're not alone. Many people feel the same way.

It can be concluded from the definitions above that NTs have a desire to connect emotionally. Aspies may wish to connect, but some may find this draining and confusing, especially if they're constantly nagged to spend time with their partner.

Conversations about emotional intimacy

A lack of emotional intimacy may lead to a build-up of emotions for both partners. Included below are conversations that demonstrate this.

NTS NEED TO BE RESPONSIBLE FOR THE EMOTIONAL SIDE OF THE RELATIONSHIP

Aspie: You can't expect me to be pulling the emotional side of the relationship together. It comes on your side of it.

NT: Why?

Aspie: Well, I don't have it, do I? The emotional level of the relationship depends on you because I have nothing to give. You have to make up for what I don't have. So I guess that's where I have to make up the mechanical and scientific side of things that you don't have.

NT: Wow, that's a real revelation to me. *I thought you just didn't care*, but I suppose if you can't give emotionally, I will have to 'make up the difference'. (Anon Aspie and NT 2007)

'EMOTIONAL INTIMACY IS TOO HARD TO FATHOM' (ANON ASPIE 2007)

NT: Why have you given up on emotional intimacy?

Aspie: It gets too hard to fathom. It's illogical. Giving decent emotional intimacy is very hard for me. If I haven't got an empathy circuit, how am I going to give you any empathy? It's a bit like having a relationship with a cat; it can only go so far because the cat hasn't got the ability to give back what you're giving. I can give you back a *mock* version of how I interpret what I'm supposed to do. I think, 'This is probably what my partner wants.' However, if I get kicked in the teeth a few times, I guess that means I'm just not good enough, so I give up and go on to another project. (Anon Aspie and NT 2007)

CRITICIZING DECREASES EMOTIONAL INTIMACY

Consistently try to make your partner feel emotionally safe. One Aspie stated, 'You might do 12 things to increase his self-esteem, then you do *one little thing wrong* or criticize him and you've undone all the good things you did the day before' (Anon 2009).

WE REALLY NEED TO HAVE A TALK

One NT really needed to have an important discussion with her husband. Two days earlier she had a fall but hadn't told him because he was in orange zone. Even though he was in orange zone again, she decided to take a risk and talk to him anyway:

> NT wife: We need to have a talk. How about in an hour when you have wound down from work?

After an hour, the Aspie didn't come and find her, so she went to find him.

> NT: Love, I really need to talk. It seems a little strange that we're married and yet two days after I had a bad fall, you're still not aware of it. We obviously don't communicate very often or very well. How can we be close if we don't talk? Sometimes, I only need you to listen.

The husband started going into red zone, stating, 'You're always whinging at me.' She still hadn't told him the details of the fall and the pain she was experiencing as a result.

> NT: I'm not going to close this communication down here, even though you're in red zone. I need to talk to you because this is a crucial moment in our relationship. At this point, I don't really care what you say to me. I'm staying here until you listen. I'm not trying to fight with you. I want to get this point across that *we need to be a couple.*
>
> Sometimes I just *need* you there for me, not necessarily emotionally or physically. We're a team and belong together. I've finished what I want to say. I'm going away now to give you some time to think about it.

Within five minutes, he came and attempted to give her an awkward hug. They didn't say a word to each other.

> NT: Let's go and cook dinner together. (Anon 2009)

As they prepared dinner, the couple related better. Standing her ground, discussing what was on her mind and providing a distraction of cooking together were effective methods of connecting emotionally.

One AS/NT couple's story

The Aspie's story

In a relationship, the Aspie needs to feel emotionally safe. This means the NT needs to get into their partner's world and understand life from the Aspie's perspective. One way to do this is to try to understand the Special Interest, especially technology and intellectual facts that he thrives on.

THE ASPIE'S POINTS CONCERNING EMOTIONAL INTIMACY

If a person doesn't feel safe, it's unlikely they will desire intimacy of any kind. My NT partner has to 'prime' me for emotional intimacy, just like I have to 'prime' her, if I want physical intimacy. Rules that need to be followed to obtain emotional intimacy with me are:

- Speak my language.
- Be involved in similar activities.
- Be on my page.
- Show interest and understanding concerning my project.
- Ask for clarification if she doesn't understand what I'm saying.

Being married is stressful for me because:

- I don't know what's expected.
- My partner wants to be greeted when she enters the room.
- She may want some type of response, but I don't have any idea what she wants.
- I'm constantly analysing what to expect.
- I don't know the social norms.

Thoughts about long-term relationships:

- I like to discover new things.
- I become bored very quickly.
- I need to find another project to stimulate my brain.
- It's very difficult to maintain a relationship.

Reasons I stay with my partner:

- It's the moral thing to do, the rule.
- I'm committed to her.

- I like her company.
- I feel important if she depends on me for physical and financial protection.
- I don't like change. (Anon 2009)

The NT's story

One strategy I've been using lately is to avoid asking my Aspie too many questions. Another thing I've done differently is to avoid telling him to do things. These strategies were so out of character for me that he said, 'Is there something wrong?' I said, 'No, I'm just trying to be quiet like you are.' As he cuddled me in bed, he said, 'It makes me feel safe.' I believe my partner felt emotionally safe because I backed off and gave him space.

THE NT'S POINTS CONCERNING EMOTIONAL INTIMACY

- Connecting with my partner by sharing my heart – how I'm feeling and what my needs are.
- Discussing topics of interest.
- Being reassured that my concerns have been heard.
- Receiving an emotional response to what I say.
- Laughing together.
- Planning a fun activity together.
- Enjoying special moments.
- Discussing the pros and cons regarding an important decision.
- Planning our future together. (Anon 2009)

Difficulty connecting

It can be concluded from the above points that the NT craved to connect emotionally, whereas the Aspie was more concerned with stability and rules. The challenge is joining these perspectives together to create a 'win–win' situation for each individual. Both partners need to make an effort to change. If the NT alters the way they relate to their partner, the Aspie may not believe at first that the NT has truly changed. If the new behaviour is consistent over a sustained period of time, the Aspie is more likely to be interested in connecting emotionally with the NT.

Insecurity, coupled with constant anxiety and low self-esteem, may hinder connecting with their partner. It can't be stressed enough that Aspies require genuine praise to reassure them that they're doing well with intimacy, whether emotional or sexual. Fear of failure in both areas is very real for Aspies.

If your partner opens up or is emotionally vulnerable with you, never laugh or belittle them. Encourage them with great gentleness because it's a rare gift or moment. They need to trust you. It's vital that you show respect as it's very unusual for an Aspie to open up. If a close moment occurs, cherish it and build on it. Let other things slide, stop what you're doing and encourage the Aspie to feel emotionally safe with you. Focus in gently on the fact that they're opening up.

Ideas to improve emotional intimacy

If you desire emotional intimacy, your relationship needs to have a firm foundation. As with anything, building a stronger relationship takes time and effort, but the dividends pay off! Suggestions to improve intimacy:

- 'Let go of the dream.'

- Remember, no expectations = no disappointments.

- Learn how to meet each other's needs. Perhaps you could say to your partner, 'What can I do to make you feel loved?'

- Explain to the Aspie what to do for you emotionally. An example is, 'I need you to hold me while I cry.'

Sexual intimacy

Because of the problem with emotional intimacy, it sometimes follows that sexual intimacy can be an issue. This is one Aspie's comment: 'Aspies like to have their personal space. When the NT wants to be intimate, it's difficult for the Aspie to connect' (Anon 2009).

Every Aspie is unique and has different needs, so the rules and comments here are not specific to all. Some NT partners have found that the following statements apply to their relationship:

- Sex can be overwhelming for the Aspie because it's about communication and emotions. Often, they may be at a loss about what to do next.

- Aspies may need step-by-step instructions of what to do, either through their partner or a book.

- The physical connection may take precedence over the emotional connection. The reason might be that they find emotional intimacy difficult and intimidating.

- If the NT sets the 'rules' prior to sex, sexual fulfilment and, at times, the emotional connection can be achieved.

- NTs who had no 'rules' before they had sex found it difficult to teach their partners new things after years of being together because Aspies don't like 'rules' being changed. Too many rules may dampen spontaneity.

- Firm or light back massage prior to sex may relax the Aspie and decrease their anxiety.

- Two extremes exist on the 'sexual continuum' of Aspies. They either desire sex a lot or not at all.

- Having sex with an Aspie is:
  - A different activity from being romantic. (Anon 2010)
  - A project for that time. The Aspie needs to be 'turned on' to that project and 'turned off' to all other projects, because they prefer to focus on one thing at a time. (Anon 2010)

- Anxiety, fear of failure and pressure to perform may affect the Aspie's ego. It's vital that partners are encouraging, supportive and non-critical, especially if the Aspie is afraid of not getting it right.

SUGGESTIONS FOR NT PARTNERS

Remember that your Aspie finds emotional intimacy overwhelming, sometimes almost impossible. Therefore, they may have a big hurdle to jump over before they're even interested in, or comfortable with sex. Let go of all expectations about having the emotional connection during sex. Instead, try to relax and have fun. If the connection happens, it's a bonus, so enjoy it.

PRACTICAL SUGGESTIONS TO DECREASE SENSORY OVERLOAD IN THE BEDROOM

If your partner has sensory problems, the following points may be helpful:

- *Visual* – Ensure lights are dim because bright lights in the bedroom might cause sensory overload.

- *Auditory* – Avoid loud noises during love making such as loud music or interruptions like phones ringing.

- *Smell* – Avoid strong perfumes, candles with fragrances and strong body odour. To reduce offensive smells, having a shower prior to sex is important.

- *Touch* – Avoid touch or massage that's too hard or too soft, depending on individual likes and dislikes. Be aware that some fabrics such as satin sheets, acrylic blankets or lacy nightwear might irritate or feel strange to the Aspie.

- *Taste* – Talk about your likes and dislikes regarding different methods of sexual intercourse with your partner. Be sensitive to their needs.

- *Communication*:

  - *During sex* – Some Aspies prefer not to talk due to the concentration required for the sexual act. This can make it difficult for women who desire 'sweet nothings', like 'You're beautiful and sexy' or 'I love you so much.'

  - *After sex* – Most women enjoy 'after-play' which is cuddling, while appreciating the experience of sexual union. Communicating positive feedback is important for women. If the man falls asleep immediately after sex, the woman can feel used and unloved.

Take away tips

- Try to be the leader of the emotional side of the relationship.

- Remember, Aspies want to experience some sort of connection.

- Explain to your partner what to do for you emotionally.

- Help your partner to feel emotionally safe.

- Be aware of the sensory issues that affect your partner.

Conclusion

Throughout this chapter, you've learned the importance of communicating and interacting on an emotional level. It's vital that both partners feel emotionally safe. Emotional and sexual intimacy may come naturally to most NTs, while being a challenge for many Aspies. Try to be patient and understanding of your partner's differences. Appreciate and enjoy the rare moments of intimacy as they're the 'glue' that holds the relationship together.

One way of discussing strategies to connect emotionally is to attend a group where encouragement, hope and validation can be found. The importance of a support group is discussed next.

Chapter 13

The Importance of a Support Group

'For many partners, just understanding *makes all the difference...
we see the difference on their faces from one month to the
next, as they begin to come to terms with their own reality
and find ways to respect themselves better.' (A point made by
Carol Grigg, from the ASPIA support group in 2009.)*

'Walking on egg shells' may be an apt description for the daily ups and
downs associated with living with an Aspie. Do you feel distressed, lonely
and that no one understands your situation? It's possible that counselling
may have been unsuccessful, especially if the counsellor was unaware that
one partner had AS. Strength, validation and help can be found through
sharing information, experiences and coping strategies with other NTs.
This chapter outlines the benefits of joining a support group to assist with
the loneliness and hurt. These groups cater for Aspies, NTs or both and
are being set up all over the world.

As you learn about AS and consider joining groups and AS
associations, you may feel overwhelmed by a mixture of negative
emotions such as sadness and anger. It's imperative to look after your
own mental health by dealing with these emotions and releasing them in
a healthy way. A support group is a safe place to do this. Through hearing
other partners' stories and being heard by NTs who understand, you may
experience feelings of tremendous relief and happiness. Hope and peace
are experienced for the first time in years, helping you to persevere for one
more day. Through listening to partners' success stories, you regain hope
that your situation can improve and your sense of identity can be found.

Benefits of joining a support group

Some of the benefits are:

- openly and freely *sharing* experiences, ideas and coping strategies
- developing wonderful *friendships* with NTs in similar situations
- feeling totally *believed, understood* and *accepted* by other NTs
- giving and receiving *empathy*
- feeling *validated*, encouraged and understood by people in similar situations
- *expressing yourself* and your opinions in a safe, confidential and non-judgemental environment
- being able to *help others* through sharing stories
- *talking and laughing* with other partners who understand
- interacting and *enjoying emotional reciprocity*
- *feeling connected and empowered* – you may feel you can conquer anything
- learning *how* the Aspie thinks and *how* to relate to them.

A lot to take in

In these groups, a wealth of helpful information is exchanged with other partners or guest speakers. This assists you in improving the way you communicate with and relate to your partner. After attending a meeting you may feel overwhelmed, especially if you have to rush off to another event. Before you know it, another day has gone and you're back in the Aspie world.

It's beneficial to network

Whether in crisis mode or not, the benefits of joining a support group are immense. Your new friends listen as you talk to your heart's content; they understand exactly where you're coming from. Strategies learned can be put into practice in between meetings. You might hear a successful story that could work with your Aspie. Then you put the plan into action. It's helpful to network with your new friends during the month through phone calls, emails or meeting for coffee. As you share with one another, an incredible sense of confidence will be felt through validation of your ideas. Pat yourself on the back occasionally for the great job you're doing as an NT partner.

Do you feel as if you're betraying your partner's trust?

Searching for help from a support group is not about betraying your partner but empowering you to learn and grow through your experiences. If your motives and intentions are to improve your relationship and not to gossip, be assured this is not betrayal.

When life gets tough, keep going to the group

Constantly 'walking on egg shells' is extremely difficult. The volatility and inconsistency of the Aspie's behaviour can result in fear, anxiety and stress for the NT. You never know what you'll face tomorrow. Due to this merry-go-round and as a result of having no energy, you may avoid the support group, especially if you're barely coping. Actually, this is when you need the group more than ever. It's when you return to the group that you realize that others care and no one is going to judge you for your actions.

It's all about trial and error

Don't forget, all Aspies and NTs are individuals and what may work for one couple, may not work for another. Sometimes, you'll have success, other times failure. It's all about experimenting with new ways of doing things. When the techniques work, you'll wish you had known about them years ago.

New partners' stories

New partners to the group share how they felt when they attended their first meeting. Be inspired by the words of a new support group member: 'It was initially like a light had gone on behind a blackened, closed door' (Anon 2009).

Another NT's story:

> I found the support group after realizing that my partner had AS. Until then, I had endured it for two years and my relationship was nearly over. I blamed myself for his shortcomings and started seeing different therapists. Friends assured me he was being a 'mere male' and that I was perhaps too 'needy'. With this in mind, I persevered and slowly, my own life, hobbies and well-being wasted away. I became an anxious person

with low self-esteem, who thought, 'If only I could handle this, all would be well.' All my normal instinctive behaviours weren't working.

It was by chance that I came across the support group and it has been the best thing for me. I had been disappointed by counsellors, who only served to tell me I was needy and had to learn to accept my partner as he was. I tried this but at a huge cost to me. None of the counsellors had knowledge of AS or the effects of living with someone that has it. It's a shame that it wasn't recognized by a professional.

Immediately on contacting the group, I was met with open arms and love and much needed understanding. I still can't believe that I've met others like me who know exactly what I'm going through. The group networks with each other and mutual support is encouraged. On the tough days, they're just a phone call away. They're positive about AS and offer tried and tested methods on how to communicate with someone with AS.

Living with someone who has AS robs the partner of a normal emotional connection and a mutual understanding of feelings and needs. I've fallen into depression, and many others are medicated or hospitalized, through the deterioration of their mental health, due to living with someone who has this condition. Many are mothers to children who also have this condition. AS is a vast and complex syndrome that demands special attention as those that live with it are lonely, isolated and misunderstood. The sad fact is that many who live with it are in total ignorance that AS is the cause of their difficulties.

Since joining the group, my self-confidence has increased. I still have anxiety but can't believe that I've found the answer. So far, the group has helped me and I would even go as far as to say, saved my life and my relationship. (Anon 2009)

Stories of hope

Partners who have attended a support group for at least six months share their stories.

NTs mean the world to Aspies

Aspies have many positive traits which are very endearing and may help us to stay with them. Although we may have struggled alone with difficulties in our relationship, we also know the good side of our Aspie that perhaps no one else has seen. They are very caring and do cute, quirky things, as well as having a good sense of humour. When a difficult period in our relationship occurs, these unique characteristics encourage us to keep trying. Knowing our partner will be like that again one day soon, we work really hard on the relationship because we still love them.

One partner shared:

A positive aspect of AS that keeps us together is that Aspies are kind people who try to understand and they're smart, bordering on genius. This eccentricity offers an unusual life of obsessive hobbies and impulsivity. They're loyal, hardworking and, deep down, we mean the world to them. (Anon 2009)

Love, laugh and live again

I was depressed and contemplated leaving my husband. Alone, sipping wine, while listening to our favourite music, I realized that I loved him and couldn't possibly leave. That was the turning point. With tears streaming down my face, the need to forgive him became evident. In my head, I knew it was right to forgive him, but it was the first time I'd felt it in my heart. *Since that day, I've told him that I love him four or five times a day.* This small change has saved our marriage. Due to my depression, I went to a doctor who prescribed antidepressants. I experienced great results from these tablets.

I'm happy now, I laugh and have hope. My husband and children have noticed a big change. The relationship with my husband has improved because *I* was willing to say, 'I need help.' Seeking assistance from a doctor and a psychologist was the integral step required to improve our marriage. For 15 years, my husband said that everything coming out of my mouth was negative. Because I'd lost my identity, as well as love for him, he hadn't heard me say, 'I love you' in a very long time. Surprised by the positive comments, his response was overwhelming. A smile would come across his face as he gave me hugs and kisses. Eventually he said, 'I love you.' The children were wondering what was happening as we weren't fighting all the time. Humour puts a smile on my husband's face and defuses the negative comments or situations.

The more positive affirmations my husband was receiving, the less frequent the meltdowns. Over time, he was more aware of the outbursts. When he did have an issue, I had an amazing new resilience. A new feeling of being back in control was present, where I would just let things go over my head. I was feeling strong; it wasn't upsetting any more. Previously, when I was extremely depressed and worn out, I had no energy left, no resilience to cope.

Finally, the resentment had gone and I'd forgiven him. Losing the dream of a happy marriage had been accepted and the grief period had finally finished. I felt *empowered* by what I'd accomplished. Currently, our relationship is far less tumultuous. My husband has only one major outburst a week, and a couple of minor ones per day, instead of one major and five minor meltdowns per day. (Anon 2008)

Backing off really works

Another NT wife shared:

When I required a lot of attention from my husband and wanted him to talk to me, he would go into meltdowns all the time because he couldn't handle talking to me. Now that I'm going out more and spending a lot of time with friends, I don't need to talk to him as much and have him listen to me all the time. As a result of me backing off, he's feeling less pressured and more relaxed. The amount of meltdowns has decreased dramatically. If he seems close to a meltdown, I now know what to do in terms of leaving him alone. The secret for me has been to avoid disturbing him and encourage him to relax or sleep. (Anon 2008)

Remember where you were

It's important to remember where you were months ago, compared to where you are now on your AS/NT relationship journey. As you move on, you tend to forget how difficult it was in the past. You've probably come a long way, but you might not be able to see that. The relationship may not be like the dream you've always wanted but it's probably much better than before you started using the techniques in this and other books.

What's your 'turning point'?

We all have different turning points. The woman in the *Love, laugh and live again* story was motivated to change through her love for her husband. The realization that she needed to forgive him was the turning point. Take a moment and ponder, 'What is *your* turning point?'

Take away tips

- Numerous benefits are gained through joining a support group – the most important is feeling validated and discovering that you're not going mad.

- Networking is beneficial.

- When life gets tough, keep going to the group.

- It's all about trial and error.

Conclusion

You're not alone in this AS/NT world. Finally someone understands! Be encouraged to attend a support group. If you can't find one in the local area, perhaps you could start your own group?

Remember, the sooner you accept that your relationship is different and look at the positives, the happier you're likely to be. Different avenues of support are available through internet forums, chat lines or emailing partners from NT support groups. Resources such as further reading and internet sites are listed at the end of this book. Numerous stories about how Aspies view the world are included in the next chapter, as well as providing insight and 'eye-opening' information regarding the Aspie's world.

Chapter 14

Entering into the Aspie's World

'I learnt that other people had minds when I was 36 years old but I still find it hard to understand this concept. I know what's in my mind, so why doesn't the other person know? Sometimes, I'm not aware of how situations are affecting NTs.' (Anon Aspie 2008)

Have you ever wondered what goes on inside your partner's brain? What are they thinking? Is there a reason for the puzzled look? Why do they become obsessed or focused on the Special Interest? This chapter explores the Aspie's style of 'black or white' thinking, mind-blindness and the significance of the Special Interest.

Many benefits are gained in understanding and entering into your Aspie's world. The figure on the following page, The Aspie's World, illustrates how one Aspie sees the world. Read from the bottom of the street sign and work your way up. This sign shows green zone at the bottom, ending with red zone at the top.

The following two sections have been inspired by an Aspie who wishes to remain anonymous (2009). The thought processes and brains of Aspies and NTs have been likened to a central processing unit (CPU).

Aspie overload

To set the scene, you and your Aspie are putting the children into the car to go grocery shopping. While this is happening, you have a fight with your partner. At the busy shopping centre, people bump into you, while you process all the associated sensory stimulants, such as visual, auditory, a range of temperatures and a variety of smells.

The Aspie's World

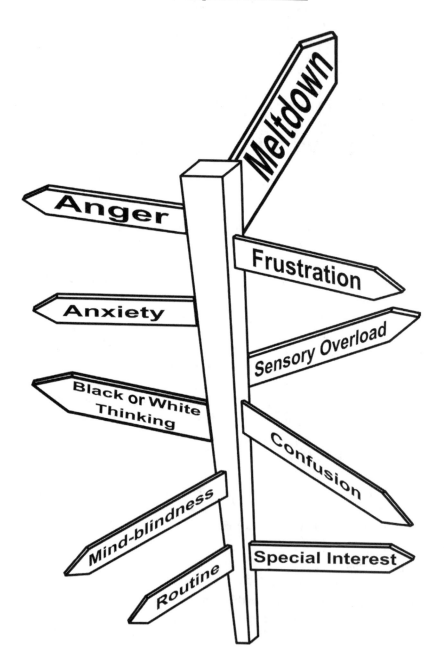

The NT brain: A quad core central processing unit (CPU)

An NT's brain is likened to a quad core computer, which is the 'brain' of a computer that processes data and sends it to the appropriate place. A quad core can process four sets of instructions simultaneously, unlike a single core where one set of instructions are processed at a time. NTs can have four pieces of information or more to process simultaneously and are able to do this with ease. Using the shopping centre scenario, imagine that you're choosing a particular grocery item. Simultaneously, you're processing thoughts and experiencing multiple sensory issues such as:

- thinking about a grieving friend
- asking your partner to deal with the children's misbehaviour (while listening to the children fighting)
- being distracted by another child pulling on your clothes
- worrying about getting your children to their club events on time.

Most NTs usually block out annoying interruptions or sensory issues. In contrast, these problems could result in some Aspies going into sensory overload because their brain is constantly bombarded by stimulants.

The Aspie's brain is likened to a single core CPU

In the same way that computers can become stuck in loops, Aspies may be caught up repeatedly processing information over and over in their mind. Sometimes, they can be perplexed by the messages and thoughts they're processing from days before.

Remember the shopping centre scenario. While the Aspie is analysing the argument that took place in the morning with their partner, they have four new pieces of sensory information *demanding* to be processed simultaneously. These new distractions *can't* be analysed immediately because the Aspie is trying to work through the argument. Frustration builds and meltdowns can occur. The Aspie may be calm, then suddenly very angry within a few seconds. Look at The Aspie's Brain: A Central Processing Unit (Single Core) on the following page to view one Aspie's perspective of how they process information.

The Aspie's Brain:
A Central Processing Unit (Single Core)

This is one Aspie's perspective of sensory overload in a shopping centre.

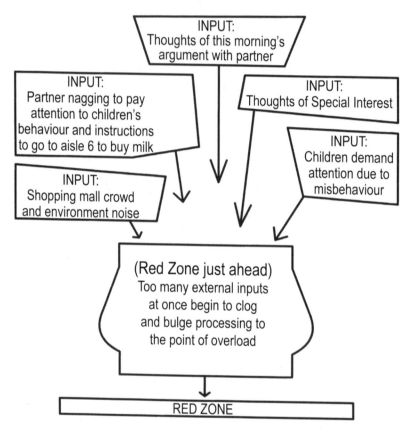

The Aspie is trying to cope with sensory overload which includes noise, crowds, their partner nagging with multiple instructions and the children demanding attention. The Aspie still hasn't processed the argument with their partner. Thoughts of the Special Interest help calm them down. It's imperative that the NT show their partner empathy as well as speaking calmly and providing space.

Insights into the Aspie's brain

As mentioned in Chapter 7, Aspies have structural and functional differences in their brain. In *The Complete Guide to Asperger's Syndrome*, Tony Attwood explains that because of these differences, understanding and regulation of emotions can be a problem. Processing thoughts and remembering information can also be difficult.

Does your partner struggle with organizing, planning and remembering events or appointments? This skill of executive functioning is impaired in Aspies (see Chapter 5). Ashley Stanford talks about this topic in her book, *Asperger Syndrome and Long-Term Relationships*. This book is highly recommended as it's a real 'eye-opener', especially the section on 'will do/won't do' activities. It's helpful to learn *why* your Aspie may have difficulty with starting some tasks. Stanford explains in her book that predictable and routine tasks, such as vacuuming and mowing, are 'will do' tasks. She also mentions that 'won't do' tasks may be avoided by Aspies because they require planning and organizing, for example, paying the children's school fees.

My brain becomes stuck

An Aspie shared:

> When I have to begin something new, my brain needs a kick-start. I don't know how or what to do to start the project. I feel lost, totally inadequate and have no idea of how to start. Then, when I finally begin, the *focus* side takes over. I just go like a 'bull at a gate' and bingo, I'm right as rain. It's just that initial start; I can never, ever get the initial start of anything. As a result, I have no confidence in my ability. The same thing happens when I'm around people. A blockage occurs and I don't know how to start a conversation. Once it starts, I end up pretty much okay. I continue on and make some sort of decent discussion out of it. (Anon 2008)

Aspies process one thing at a time

An Aspie shared how he processes his thoughts:

> An Aspie may have difficulty sending messages to their brain and analysing them. The messages have trouble passing through their brain quickly enough, resulting in increased frustration. The demand on the Aspie to hurry up and answer questions and resolve conflicts is really stressful. (Anon 2009)

Impulsivity

In *The Complete Guide to Asperger's Syndrome*, Tony Attwood describes being impulsive as a sign of impaired executive function. One Aspie shared the reason for being impulsive:

> If something is on my mind and I don't deal with it immediately, or make amends, I forget about it. This causes even greater frustration, so I always need to be on top of things and remember to do things straight away, otherwise I'll forget and that infuriates me. (Anon 2008)

Logical and organized

Aspies sometimes have the ability to separate their emotions from a situation. This is a positive trait and can be invaluable in the case of an emergency, such as a motor vehicle accident. An Aspie can assist by using logic because at that moment they can separate their emotions from the circumstances. In a similar situation, some NTs can be overcome by emotions such as grief and shock which may hinder their logical, decision-making processes.

'Black or white' thinking

Your partner sees things in *black or white*. They may not realize that you see things differently. Here are some scenarios that highlight black or white thinking.

STORY A: YOUR LOGIC DOESN'T MAKE ANY SENSE

One NT's experience:

> When we encounter misunderstandings, he raises his voice and says things like, 'I thought we discussed this issue and found a solution, so that's the end of the discussion. Why do you have to keep going on and on about it? Your logic doesn't make any sense. Why can't you see that? It's logical. Why don't you have any logic? You're a professional with a degree. How did you get a degree if you don't have any logic?'(Anon 2007)

STORY B: STEERING WHEEL LOCKS SHOULD BE *ALL* BLACK OR BLACK AND RED

An NT shared:

> I was at the shops, choosing a steering wheel lock for my car. Blue would be nice for a change, I thought, so that's the colour I bought. When I came

home and showed my Aspie, he said, 'Club-locks should only be *all* black or black and red.' I replied, 'I knew this would happen. It's *my* car and *I* should be allowed to choose the colour *I* want.' He said, 'OK, but every time I use it, I'll wish you got the black and red one.' I'd already opened the packet, when he mentioned it again. I was exhausted and couldn't be bothered arguing over a car lock, so I said to him, 'Look, if you don't like it, go back to the store and change it.'

Immediately, he went back to the store and changed it to red and black. Things always seem to go his way. Even though I was feeling a little annoyed, I would much rather give up something I want, to keep the peace. After all, it would be easier than being reminded *every* day that I bought the 'wrong' colour. (Anon 2007)

Mind-blindness

Recall the definition from Ashley Stanford in her book, *Asperger Syndrome and Long-Term Relationships*: mind-blindness is 'the *inability* to see others as having their own *state* of mind (p.273).' One Aspie said that, 'The people become irrelevant, logic wins out; the only way to do something is my way, the logical way' (Anon 2008).

An Aspie explained:

Aspies don't understand, or have difficulty in understanding, that there's something outside of them. Some are in their own little world and may think, 'I don't feel upset, so why does the other person feel upset?' They might not be aware of boundaries because they're not aware that other people have minds. If I think something a certain way, then why doesn't the other person think the same way? (Anon 2009)

Examples of mind-blindness
STORY 1: WHAT?! YOU HAVE A MIND?

One NT partner shared:

After a nice evening together, my Aspie was helping me with something and he said, 'You're so stupid, you're so ignorant.'

I calmly said, 'Now, that's your opinion and it's abusive. Do you realize that I have a mind too?'

He said, 'What?'

I repeated myself and added, 'I think differently to you.'

He said, 'No, you're stupid.'

I said calmly, 'No, that's your opinion about this situation. I really would appreciate it if you would stop calling me abusive names.'

He said, 'But you're ignorant.'

I said, 'That's another abusive word.'

Then I said, 'I have a mind like you. Can you understand that? I have different thoughts and opinions to you. You're trying to tell me that what I'm thinking isn't right. Well, I have a different opinion to you.'

He said, with a shocked look on his face, 'What?! What?!'

I said, 'I'm not saying you must have the *same* opinion as me but that I'm entitled to *my* opinion. Will you think about that?'

He said, 'All right.' It took a long time for the concept to sink in.

I was very excited by this rare, significant moment, where the light had finally gone on. I stopped talking, so that he could have some more time to digest the information. (Anon 2009)

STORY 2: THAT'S NOT HOW YOU CUT A TOMATO

An NT wife shared:

The more I researched about AS, the more I understood how my husband's brain worked. Our life was quite stressful. He didn't seem to understand my point of view, which led me to think that something was wrong with him. A fight over a tomato, which led to his diagnosis, was the 'straw that broke the camel's back'.

Arriving home from work one day, I noticed that my Aspie had hurt his finger. He was preparing dinner so I offered to cut the tomato for him. He expected me to cut the tomato *his* way. I cut it a different way, thinking we were going to have it in tacos. With a frustrated look on his face, he yelled at me, 'That's not the way you cut a tomato.' I felt shocked and extremely upset by his outburst and couldn't believe the way he was berating me. With deliberation, I placed the knife on the worktop and said, 'You can do it yourself then. I'm not going to fight with you over a tomato.'

Walking away from the situation, I decided that I'd had enough of these episodes; I wasn't going to fight with him any more about something so trivial. With mixed emotions and heart racing, the realization of what I'd done engulfed me. I felt proud of myself, but at the same time ambivalent. I wasn't going to allow his frustration to upset me any more.

The next day I went to visit my friend who has a son with AS and told her this story. She said, 'You did the right thing. It's best to walk away, distance yourself from him.' My friend explained what 'mind-blind' means; that my husband only sees *his* way of cutting a tomato. She added, 'He really can't see your point of view.' I was pleased that I had gained this knowledge. It explained the reason for the frequent misunderstandings. (Anon 2007)

STORY 3: I DON'T WANT ICE, SO SHE WON'T WANT ICE

An NT shared:

My partner and I went to a Mexican restaurant for dinner. I asked him if he could get me some water from the bar. When returning from the bar, he walked past me carrying a flask of water and two glasses. He then went outside and threw something in the garden. I thought that he must think there was a bin in the garden. When he returned to the table, I asked him what he threw in the rubbish bin. He said, 'Nothing. I threw ice in the garden.' Considering we were in a posh restaurant, I thought that was an odd thing to do. My Aspie disagreed and said it was the logical thing to do because he didn't want ice in his water. I said, 'Did you think to ask me if *I* wanted ice?' (Anon 2007)

What an interesting scenario where the Aspie decided to discard the ice from both glasses because he didn't want ice. This is an example of mind-blindness. It could be seen as a selfish action because the NT may have wanted ice in her water. This is an example of how Aspies sometimes don't understand social etiquette. Aspies may seem selfish but often they're not; they're just mind-blind.

STORY 4: CAMPING

An NT shared:

Shortly after he was diagnosed with AS, we were camping in our station wagon, somewhere in New South Wales. During the night, my partner opened the window, without asking my permission. When I saw the window open, I became annoyed, as I'm usually bitten by mozzies. Irritated, I looked for the insect repellent in the dark which I sprayed on myself. In the morning I said to him, 'Can I please just say one thing? When you want to open the window in the night, can you ask me first so I can put some insect repellent on?' He became really upset in response to my question and said, 'Go to hell, I can't cope any more.' Normally I would be upset by the way he spoke to me, but I just let it go. Ten minutes later, he said, 'It was hot last night, so I opened the window. I had an

Asperger's moment. I was mind-blind to your needs.' It's encouraging to see that he accepts his AS and is sometimes willing to admit when he's wrong. (Anon 2007)

STORY 5: GETTING A JOB

An Aspie shared:

I have 'blindness' about how to obtain a job: what to do, how to do it, where to go, how to sell myself. The possibility of rejection might have something to do with it. Why can't I be successful the first time? Why do I have to go for a job many times? It doesn't make any logical sense to keep applying for jobs and being rejected. Why can't I go for an interview and be accepted and that's the end of it? (Anon 2008)

STORY 6: THE PUPPET SHOW

An Aspie shared:

When I was 12 years old, I wanted to help raise money at the school fete. I decided to create a puppet show. This became my Special Interest, spending hours building the set and making the puppets. I also recorded my voice. The tape recorder blared out at full volume, 'Come and see the puppet show.' Much to my disappointment, no one came. A few days later I spoke to my teacher about it. She said, 'Why didn't you have it announced over the loud speaker? Then people at the fete would have known the puppet show was on.'

It just didn't occur to me that others might be willing to help. I now realize that is mind-blindness to the max. With everything I do, the situation is similar. If I can't do it myself, then in my mind, it can't be done. I don't realize it's possible to ask for someone's assistance. I just can't see past myself. Ever since this event, feelings of rejection and failure have set in and affected me for years. (Anon 2008)

It didn't occur to this Aspie to inform people at the fete that he was having a puppet show. Maybe he thought people would know to come; he knows, so he thinks others know. It's clear that this child was in his own little world, the world of the Special Interest.

The benefits of the Special Interest

Provides focus

Sometimes, the Aspie needs motivation to start a project. After their brain kick-starts, they're in 'focus mode'. Once your partner has started a project, it's difficult to pull them away from it. The ability to concentrate on a task until completion is a positive trait of Aspies. If your partner is focused, they can achieve great things.

Tip: Incorporate the Aspie's skills of focusing (on the Special Interest) into planning an event. If your partner has a Special Interest in maps or history, involve them in organizing the family holiday.

Contributes to self-identity

- Gives purpose.

- Brings excitement through learning and discovering why something happens and what makes it work.

- Provides a challenge.

- Fuses with self. A female Aspie shared, 'The *special interest* fuses with me. It allows for a complete and relaxed sense of who I am' (Anon 2009). A male Aspie stated, 'When I spend time on my project, it becomes part of me' (Anon 2008).

Increases self-esteem

- Particularly when praise is received from others.

- When the challenge is conquered, an exhilarating feeling is experienced.

Encourages expression of creative abilities

- Develops other abilities while completing the task at hand.

- Their project is an expression of themselves.

Provides pleasure

An Aspie shared his story:

> When you finish the special project, you gain a bit of an ego boost, self-esteem boost. I become lost in my own little world. Film and video are my Special Interest. I find pleasure in creating something and sinking myself

into it. I enjoy the end of the video editing project when I can stand back and say, 'Wow, that looks good.' Then I spend 70 hours editing it, another 70 hours doing all the fine tuning and another 70 hours tweaking it. Time just disappears, nobody annoys me. The only hassle I have is when the computer breaks down or has a little glitch in it somewhere. Computers I can control; people I can't. Fixing computers is what I do well. I can't understand people, so I just steer clear of them. They have illogical ways of thinking. (Anon 2008)

The above story points out how engrossed the Aspie can become in the Special Interest.

Healthy boundaries and the Special Interest

Anyone can do things to the extreme at times. However, forgetting to drink, eat and sleep are signs that the Aspie is neglecting their basic needs or family and work responsibilities. It's understandable that the NT becomes concerned if the Aspie spends an excessive amount of time (continuously, not a few days) on their Special Interest. In these cases, boundaries must be put into place. Even though it's necessary to determine acceptable limits in relation to the Special Interest, it's also extremely important for the NT to respect their partner's *need* for this time alone. By backing off and letting their partner enjoy the Special Interest within healthy limits, the NT is assisting the Aspie to feel emotionally secure.

Help your partner feel emotionally safe

At first, if you're feeling exhausted and unloved, it can be really difficult to encourage the Aspie's Special Interest. However, if you're able to persevere with this, it's likely that your partner will feel emotionally secure and start to believe that you love and care for them. It's up to you to take the first step in helping your partner to feel emotionally safe. As a result of your concern for their very real need for the Special Interest, the Aspie may slowly start to show that they care about you in little ways, resulting in some enjoyable, happy times together. This fulfils love and belonging needs for both of you, as suggested by Maslow in Chapter 10.

Aspies, please note

When it comes to the amount of time spent on the Special Interest, NTs may have concerns, especially if it's a 'detrimental' Special Interest, such as gambling or pornography. Perhaps they're just worried for your physical and emotional well-being, as well as how the Special Interest has an impact on finances and the welfare of the rest of the family. Personal and couple counselling may be beneficial in these situations.

Conclusion

Aspies have difficulty with mind-blindness and 'black or white' thinking. It's important that you assist them by being patient, understanding and empathic. Entering into the Aspie's world is one way to comprehend their struggles.

This poem illustrates how one NT entered into her Aspie's world:

> He smiled at me, much like the time our eyes first met.
> With a quiet hesitation, he looked to me for reassurance and support
> As he launched into his story.
> Not an easy thing for him to do in front of a crowd,
> Not his favourite time or place to be.
> Nothing like the space and freedom of the sea and sailing he so dearly loved.
> The Special Interest that freed him from anxiety and doubt,
> That fed his heart and soul and brought him peace.
> I smiled back and firmly, gently, touched his hand.
> (Anon NT, married for 27 years to an Aspie)

The value of the Aspie's Special Interest can't be stressed enough. If it provides pleasure to the Aspie, no one has a right to rob them of this exhilarating feeling. Wouldn't it be wonderful if your partner entered into *your* world by encouraging your passion? Perhaps you could have a discussion with them about your needs, goals and dreams. The importance of appreciating each other's positive traits is highlighted in the final chapter, *The Unique Partnership*.

Chapter 15

The Unique Partnership

'Love does not consist in gazing at each other but in looking together in the same direction.' (from God's Little Instruction Book on Love, *published by Honor Books*)

Consider why you were first attracted to your Aspie. Was it because they were quiet, genuine, kind, intelligent or quirky? Why do you think your partner fell in love with you? Was it because you're an extremely caring, intuitive and social person? You were drawn to your partner and they were drawn to you. Opposites attract.

Over time, the characteristics that attracted you may have become hidden in frequent misunderstandings, often leading to constant meltdowns. No relationship is perfect. Living with an Aspie is not easy because they can be arrogant and rarely let the NT 'off the hook' for mistakes made. Likewise, living with an NT has its drawbacks for an Aspie, due to their apparent 'illogical and over-emotional nature' (Anon Aspie 2009).

The unique AS/NT relationship will challenge you beyond what you ever thought possible, though many positives can be found. If both partners are willing to try to understand each other's world, despite being on two different wavelengths, this unique partnership *can* be successful. It's a fact that the responsibility for making an AS/NT relationship work will fall heavily on the NT. The collective experience of NT partners in this book shows that once a full understanding of AS is reached, the NT usually makes adjustments. Such compromise by the NT is hard, but rewarding. As a result of this effort, their Aspie partner may slowly change.

This chapter endeavours to capture the essence of the AS/NT relationship. Concepts such as 'opposites attract', teamwork and companionship are discussed. Considering that this chapter is about your *relationship*, it's written to both the Aspie and the NT. Perhaps you could read this chapter together?

Liken your relationship to a dual-control car

Imagine a driving instructor's car that has dual controls. In this car, the driving instructor guides the learner through the difficult and unknown situations, as well as being there for support when needed.

Liken this car to the AS/NT partnership, in which the couple work together as a team. The Aspie is driving the car, while the NT navigates and gently steers the couple in the right direction. The NT is in the passenger seat, interpreting and supporting them through stressful situations and communication difficulties.

Aspies, it's vital that you put your trust in the NT to guide and assist you, especially in the emotional and social terrain. NTs, consider the Aspie's intellectual and logical contributions to the relationship. It's really important that you both value the qualities of your partner and encourage each other to pursue their own hobbies and passions, independently of one another.

Use this manual

This book is a relationship manual, written to guide you in negotiating the maze of intimacy. The four vital keys are: learn about AS, 'let go of expectations', maintain your 'energy cup' and aim for 'quick recovery time'.

Do opposites attract?

In an AS/NT partnership, the Aspie and 'extreme' NT may be from opposite ends of the social and empathy spectrum, as described by Tony Attwood in his book, *The Complete Guide to Asperger's Syndrome*. Add the logical level-headedness of the Aspie to the emotional, caring, empathic nature of the 'extreme' NT and you have the basis for a great relationship.

You're a team

Teamwork involves working with your partner's differences in a positive way. It's a waste of time working against them. Are you able to allow each other the space required to be individuals, while participating in regular, enjoyable activities together?

Instead of complaining, accept that the relationship isn't conventional. To build a successful relationship, *both* partners need to focus on self-improvement. Be open and honest about your part in the relationship difficulties. Professional help from an AS specialist is often necessary when unresolved issues of a sensitive and complex nature are 'swept under the carpet'. Past grievances regarding family of origin, finance, parenting, mental health issues or addictions need to be discussed. It's also important to deal with current issues.

Some people oppose counselling because of the inherent need to be honest and expose one's weaknesses and faults. Such openness, however, is part of healing. Counselling can be extremely helpful in working through the grief and healing processes. Mutual compromise is also needed. If one partner won't seek help or meet the other half way, don't give up. You can still work on yourself. Remember, you can only change yourself, you can't change another person.

One positive aspect of being in an AS/NT relationship is that you can work as a team. The Aspie may remain calm in a crisis and provide practical assistance, while the NT may empathize with the person going through the crisis by comforting them emotionally. If your child falls off his bike, the Aspie may fix the bike or put a sticking plaster on the wound while the NT hugs and soothes the child.

Perseverance

As with any relationship, time and perseverance are necessary. First, make it a priority to spend some quality time together. Start by talking about any areas of your relationship that require improvement. Jot down these areas, including goals that are realistic and achievable within a reasonable time-frame. Write down how these goals can be achieved, for example, both partners may need to compromise in order to spend some quality time with each other.

Second, patiently work together to meet your goals. Practise the relevant strategies found in this book that relate directly to these goals. If communication is an area of difficulty for example, both partners could try to implement the ideas found in Chapter 6. It's really exciting when, *together*, you devise your own personal strategies that actually work!

Companionship

If you look past the meltdowns, most AS/NT couples will find that they have companionship. Being each other's best friend will hold you together through shared struggles. Winnie Lau (2009), a Clinical Psychologist from the Minds and Hearts Clinic in Brisbane, Australia, agreed that companionship is at the heart of the AS/NT partnership. She wrote:

> I've seen many AS/NT couples who maintain a mutually edifying relationship with companionship at the centre. These couples continuously admire and benefit from each other's qualities that are complementary to their own. For example, an Aspie spouse can help his/her spouse to make rational decisions during emergencies, offer well-informed advice on certain subjects, provide objective views on interpersonal affairs, observe new ways of solving a problem and so on. Many NTs find their Aspie partner's bravery in sticking to his/her convictions and freedom from conforming to unhelpful 'social norms' admirable.
>
> On the other hand, Aspies need support from their NT spouse in areas such as considering other's perspectives, reading unspoken intentions, prioritizing and so on. Often, NTs can make a significant difference to their Aspie partner's functioning by providing support to their emotion management, especially in relation to anxiety. The need for 'extra care' when an Aspie is anxious is similar to how NTs require much more input to maintain their social and emotional needs. Ultimately, it's about give and take. (Personal Communication)

Appreciate your partner's positives

Praise is often lacking in an AS/NT relationship. Encourage your loved one's positive qualities by praising them for their delightful and unique traits.

To NTs

Aspies have an awe-inspiring intelligence and a wealth of knowledge about general topics, as well as their Special Interests. They're very logical in their thinking, which may exceed that of the NT. Logical thinking is vital in situations where immediate problem solving is required. As mentioned earlier, the invaluable help of the Aspie in a crisis is astounding.

In contrast, an NT can have difficulty coping with the emotional content of a situation. Thank the Aspie when they help you in a practical way and compliment them when they succeed at reading your emotions, attempt to comfort you or do well in a social situation. It's vital to accept the Aspie the way they are and avoid judging or having unrealistic expectations of them.

To Aspies

Do you find interpreting emotions and social situations difficult? Ask the NT to assist you, particularly if you're feeling stressed or overwhelmed. NTs are very good at knowing when you're anxious, frustrated or angry and have a greater ability to know the appropriate behaviour in a social situation. It's important to value NTs for all their love, help, forgiveness and the way they patiently calm you down during or after meltdowns. They're extremely caring, empathic people, who are very understanding of your needs.

NTs perform a lot of 'behind-the-scenes' roles that an Aspie may not even notice, such as being the organizer, peacemaker for you and other family members, social and emotional interpreter, encourager and many more. They're worthy of much praise for their dedication and perseverance for changing to meet your needs and finding answers to the relationship issues.

PRACTICAL IDEAS FOR ASPIES

Listening attentively is of great importance when the NT is sharing their heart with you. Sometimes, NTs just need to talk about their day; they don't necessarily need a solution. If they look emotional or busy, ask them, 'Is there anything I can do to help?' Buying a gift or giving a hug may help your partner to feel better if they're upset.

What are the positive attributes of your partner?

Both partners have many exceptional traits that can assist their loved one on a daily basis. Instead of focusing on the negatives, take a step back and look at your partner's positive attributes.

To NTs

Write down some positive qualities of your Aspie. Listed below are some ideas. Perhaps you can add more?

- genuine – what you see is what you get
- loyal

- practical
- reliable
- hard working
- intelligent
- stable
- logical
- focused and determined
- honest.

To Aspies

Write down some of the positive qualities of your NT. Listed below are some ideas. Please add more.

- understanding
- intuitive
- good listener
- kind and caring
- patient
- emotionally strong
- social
- encouraging
- empathic
- good organizers.

Let's recap

Throughout this book, you've gained numerous insights regarding the dynamics of the AS/NT relationship. Let's revisit the main points. Take a few moments to answer 'yes' or 'no' to the following:

- Are you respectful of each other's differences?
- Do you have any expectations of your partner?
- Is your energy cup at least three-quarters full and do you have a reserve for emergencies?

- Are you letting go of control and allowing your partner to pursue their dreams, gifts and talents?

- Has communication improved?

- Do you help each other to understand the differences in your thinking?

- Do you assist your partner in dealing with their emotions?

- Do you walk away if you're being abused?

- Are you taking proactive steps to maintain your energy?

- Are you starting to regain your identity?

If the answer to some of these questions is 'yes', congratulations! You've achieved a great deal and are headed in the right direction. Don't worry if you're still working on some areas. Eventually, these insights will become second nature. Regardless of how long you've known about AS, if you grasp these concepts and relevant strategies, you'll learn something new almost every day. It takes time, patience and practice to implement these new techniques. With effort from both of you, a positive difference can be made in your relationship.

Conclusion

Negotiating the maze of intimacy is a continual process of two steps forward, one step back. The four vital keys are: learn about AS, 'let go of expectations', maintain your 'energy cup' and aim for 'quick recovery time'.

Remember the two-for-one deal: two rejuvenating activities for one draining activity. It's imperative that you place a high priority on meeting *your* needs and schedule fulfilling relaxation time into your life. This leaves you with enough energy for emergencies. Once you have energy, you're ready to regain your identity. As this is regained and communication with your partner begins to improve, connecting will become easier.

Connecting with Your Asperger Partner commenced with the quote 'Sometimes what seems like the darkest step we've ever been on comes just before the brightest light we've ever experienced' (from p.33 of *Just Enough Light for the Step I'm On* by Stormie Omartian). You may have been through many dark hours. Be encouraged, implementing the strategies recommended in this book gives you hope to reach the light at the end of the tunnel. Now is the time to enjoy this challenging and rewarding partnership.

The Ten Golden Keys to Connecting

1. Learn about AS.

2. 'Let go of expectations.'

3. Maintain your 'energy cup'.

4. Aim for 'quick recovery time'.

5. Refer to *The Steps to Self-discovery and Connecting* in Chapter 1.

6. Refer to *In the Zone Charts* in Chapter 9.

7. Regain your identity.

8. Experiment with new ways of connecting emotionally and intimately.

9. Enter into each other's world – encourage the Special Interest or passion.

10. Focus on each other's positive traits and be proud that you're a part of this extraordinary and unique partnership.

Afterword

The Author's Story

'To have a healthy relationship with God or anyone else,
I must not expect anything.' (Graham Weston 1997)

I was the project

Our relationship is unique and we have a beautiful romantic story! I'm not sure about the term 'love at first sight' being true, but for ten years our lives have been connected providentially. The moment we met in 1998, it was 'as if it was meant to be'. Our eyes locked together when we were introduced to each other at church. Graham was unshaven, dressed in a leather jacket and daggy ripped jeans, carrying a motorbike helmet. Not my idea of appealing, but I looked past his outward appearance and thought he was 'all right'. That night, Graham went home and wrote this beautiful passage.

'Louise's Prophecy'

> When I met you tonight, for the first time I foresaw a vision of an angel. An Angel who is diligently mending from a broken heart, in which I have a desire to reward her efforts with grace and honour, she so richly deserves. Respecting her for the persistent one she is. A shattered innocence who strove to forgive and love again.

> While your future serenity flooded my soul my eyes were fixed to your aura of repose, which seeks to enter your heart. I felt the purity of restored innocence shine from the merciful heart that waits to reward your persistence to reach the 'forgiving past'.

Tonight, your smile extolled your inner beauty you wish to share as your glance illuminated brightly into my soul capturing it for but a brief moment. I look forward to the possibility of being within your presence again; hoping to experience your friendship as it grows into a cloudless heart of love and understanding.

© *Graham Weston 1998*

I was careful not to make much of this beautiful passage but we did fall in love a few months later. Due to our Christian beliefs, it was decided that we wouldn't have a sexual relationship prior to marriage. Our first kiss and everything beyond that would happen on our wedding day. Now that I know about AS, I realize why he had such restraint. I was the project; the Special Interest. Once Graham makes a decision, he finds it difficult to change his mind. The rule he adhered to was, 'No kissing until the wedding day.'

Within three days of courting, we believed God revealed to us individually that we were to marry. We kept this secret in our hearts for three long weeks and then shared our divine message with each other. Graham had a checklist of 73 criteria for a wife and I met every one of them. Our courtship was an exciting 11 months where Graham swept me off my feet by surprising me with numerous love letters and poems, as well as creating precious memories. I had constant palpitations from the anticipation of seeing him. The palpitations disappeared on the wedding day.

Graham and I had excellent communication skills during our courtship. Within two weeks of knowing each other, we'd shared our deepest secrets. This gave us emotional closeness. We believed that spiritual intimacy would lead to emotional intimacy and in turn become physical intimacy. Consequently, a lot of time was spent talking. He made me laugh; the little idiosyncrasies and beautiful way he treated me were so admirable. Some of the virtues that drew me to Graham were his adventurous spirit, determination to succeed, attention to detail and ability to focus on a job until completion.

Anxiety, frustration and anger are a few of the negative AS traits that Graham experiences. On reflection, I recall a couple of occasions when I saw him angry. It didn't bother me as I thought, 'No one is perfect.' One time, I went to a photo shop to have some film developed. While I was talking to the assistant, Graham came bounding in, took over and told the woman exactly what I wanted. Thinking this behaviour a bit odd, I named it, 'over-the-top syndrome'. This was our first fight and we successfully resolved the conflict. It wasn't until two weeks before the wedding that I noticed he would raise his voice at times. This would occur during stressful moments or when more people were around. An example of this was when his children from a previous marriage came to stay. When the children misbehaved, Graham would raise his voice. Not knowing much about children, I thought that was the usual response.

In retrospect, I can see the Asperger qualities that drew me to Graham – his attention to detail, his loyalty, honesty, kindness and eagerness to repair things for me. In him, I had what most women could only dream of. Whenever I saw him, I would jump into his arms and he would spin me around. It was just so beautiful, so wonderful!

After a difficult first marriage that didn't really have much of a courtship, I couldn't believe that I'd met someone so charming and that we could be so incredibly happy. Graham treated me like a lady. Now, how many men out there still open the car door or pull out a chair for a woman? Not many! I feel very grateful that he still does these special things for me even to this day. Graham makes me feel like I'm worth a million dollars.

Early married life

The wedding day was perfect, the first kiss a little embarrassing in front of all those people. The initial few weeks of our marriage proved to be very difficult. Graham would focus on the computer which was in our bedroom, spending hours on a project. I remember thinking, 'It would be nice to have some affection, intimacy or quality time together.' Graham didn't understand this and I considered this to be unusual. Intuitively, I knew something was wrong, but failed to understand what. The lack of attention was such an issue that I remember buying a book called *400 Ways to Say I Love You*. A family member who saw me reading this said, 'You shouldn't need that – you've only been married for three weeks.'

We had different expectations of what marriage was all about. I had also become a step mother to Grahams's children, a boy aged nine and a girl aged eight (now 21 and 19), who taught me a lot about life. They're beautiful children. I love them like they're my own and wouldn't swap them for the world.

One day is vivid in my mind, when I needed Graham to help me with parenting. He was focused on establishing our yard, but I needed his attention and help with the children. As he couldn't be in two places at once, this resulted in him becoming confused and frustrated. Graham has since told me his reasoning that day was, 'She wants me to do the garden but she wants me inside. Which is most important? What's her problem; can't she just sort the children out herself?' Over time, the more I said 'Come inside,' the more he'd become angry and withdraw. If I badgered, questioned or wallowed in self-pity, he would put up more walls. Layer upon layer was forming around him and I couldn't get through. Our relationship lacked emotional intimacy. After four years of marriage, Graham thought about ending the relationship. Thankfully, his Aspie loyalty prevented him from leaving me.

Since Graham has been diagnosed with AS, I have a deeper understanding of what motivates him. Special Interests inspire him by providing a deep sense of personal satisfaction, achievement and self-worth.

Finding out about AS

After seven years of marriage, I knew something was not quite right with our relationship. It took me a while to figure this out, as Graham's negative traits of AS hid behind the positives. I used to wonder why he would shout or become annoyed when his routine was interrupted. He would yell at me or at himself if he lost something or when a task wasn't completed to his expectations. In time and through self-education, I slowly became aware that these were all common traits of an Aspie.

Graham actually diagnosed himself, but for one year we didn't know the best way to obtain a formal diagnosis. I decided to write this book because public awareness of AS was lacking. It has been a worthwhile journey, resulting in both of us gaining theoretical and practical knowledge. Subsequently, Graham's insight into AS has enabled him to tell me when he is stressed. I now understand that he requires space and relaxes by engaging in and mastering his Special Interest.

The more I researched, the more I realized we were going around in circles. Reading Katrin Bentley's book *Alone Together*, particularly the chapter on 'The Energy Theory', changed my life. Unaware of the energy battle that existed, I learnt from the book that four things can drain energy in a relationship: anger, withdrawal, self-pity and demands or questioning. It dawned on me that this was happening in our marriage. I was in 'self-pity and questioning mode' and Graham was in 'anger and withdrawal mode'. I discussed this new theory with Graham and he agreed that this was evident in our marriage. Even though I'd 'let go', I had a *lot* more changing to do.

Changes I have made

Realizing that Aspies find change difficult, I explored ways to improve our situation. Working on *me* was effective in improving our marriage. Since *I've changed*, Graham is less verbally abusive and has fewer meltdowns.

Since the diagnosis of AS, I've learned to become more flexible, resulting in an improvement in our relationship. It's taken time and much effort to change but it's been worth it. I'm very grateful that I have a lovely husband. Graham is starting to change, because I've changed. He's actually able to be himself now. One significant comment he made was, 'It's always darkest before the dawn.' As a joke, I replied, 'Yeah, it was *very* dark before it "dawned on me" that I had to change.' Another statement he made was, 'If you want to change the world, guess where it starts? The NT has to change first and then maybe the Aspie will follow.'

If you think, 'Why should I change?' you're absolutely right, why should you? But then again, why shouldn't you? What's easier – being exhausted from daily misunderstandings and meltdowns or learning how to regain energy, identity and peace?

We laughed at how I used to be

One day, we were travelling in the car and Graham was driving. I was amazed at how relaxed he was all day. On the way home from our trip, he swerved quickly across the road. I told myself to keep my mouth shut and avoid criticizing him. When I looked over at Graham, he was laughing and said, 'I can't believe you didn't say anything. The "old" you would have said something about my driving and complained about how sick you felt because I swerved.' I also laughed about how I used to be.

We enjoy lovely times of connecting now

Graham is one of the most sincere and honest people I know. When I receive a phone call or text message from him, I know it comes from his heart. A treasured text he sent me which brought tears to my eyes said, 'I'm blessed to have you as my wife; you are very understanding.' How special is that? I pray that you, my reader, will cherish the special moments of connecting too.

Bibliography

Asperger Services Australia (2007) *Asperger's Syndrome...What Is It?* Brisbane: Asperger Services Australia. (Information Card.)

Aston, M. (2003) *Aspergers in Love*. London: Jessica Kingsley Publishers.

Aston, M. (2009) *The Asperger Couple's Workbook*. London: Jessica Kingsley Publishers.

Attwood, T. (2007) *The Complete Guide to Asperger's Syndrome*. London: Jessica Kingsley Publishers.

Beattie, M. (1992) *Codependent No More*. Center City: Minnesota: Hazelden (original work published in 1986).

Becvar, R.J., Canfield, B.S. and Becvar, D.S. (1997) *Group Work: Cybernetic, Constructivist and Social Constructivist Perspectives*. Denver, CO: Love Publishing Co.

Bentley, K. (2007) *Alone Together: Making an Asperger Marriage Work*. London: Jessica Kingsley Publishers.

Carlson, N., Martin, G. and Buskist, W. (2004) *Psychology*. Harlow: Pearson (first published in 2000).

Cloud, H. and Townsend, J. (1992) *Boundaries: When to Say Yes, When to Say No, To Take Control of Your Life*. Sydney: Strand Publishing.

Dolliver, R. (1981) 'Reflections on Fritz Perls's Gestalt Prayer.' *Personnel and Guidance Journal 59* (5), 311–13.

Eunson, B. (2005) *Communicating in the 21st Century*. Milton: John Wiley & Sons Australia, Ltd (first published in 2005).

Gressor, M. (2004) *Loss and Grief: Dealing With Life Crises: how to cope with bereavement, divorce, losing your job*. Sydney and Double Bay: ACP Publishing Pty Ltd and Media 21 Publishing Pty Ltd (joint publishers).

Harley, W., Jr. (2008) *Love Busters: Protecting Your Marriage from Habits That Destroy Romantic Love*. Grand Rapids, MI: Revell (first published in 1992).

Honor Books (1996) *God's Little Instruction Book on Love*. Tulsa, OK: Honor Books Inc.

Johnson, J.T. (1994) *Hidden Victims, Hidden Healers: An Eight-Stage Healing Process for Families and Friends of The Mentally Ill*. Edina, Minnesota: PEMA Publications Inc. (first published in 1988).

Kirshenbaum, M. (2003) *The Emotional Energy Factor: The Secrets High-energy People Use to Beat Emotional Fatigue*. New York: Bantum Dell, a division of Random House.

Kotzman, A. and Kotzman, M. (2007) *Listen to Me, Listen to You: A Step-by-Step Guide to Communication Skills Training*. Camberwell: Penguin books (first published in 1989). (New Expanded Edition).

Kübler-Ross, E. and Kessler, D. (2005) *On Grief and Grieving: Finding the Meaning of Grief Through the Five Stages of Loss*. London: Simon Schuster UK Ltd.

Lerner, H. (2001) *The Dance of Connection*. New York: HarperCollins Publishers.

Lovett, J. (2005) *Solutions for Adults with Asperger Syndrome*. Gloucester: Fair Winds Press.

McCabe, P., McCabe, E. and McCabe, J. (2003) *Living and Loving with Asperger Syndrome*. London: Jessica Kingsley Publishers.

Omartian, S. (2008a) 'Just enough light' in S. Omartian *Just Enough Light for the Step I'm On*. Eugene, OR: Harvest House Publishers (first published in 1999).

Omartian, S. (2008b) *Just Enough Light for the Step I'm On*. Eugene, OR: Harvest House Publishers (first published in 1999).

Sandford, J.R., Sandford, P. and Bowman, L. (2007) *Choosing Forgiveness*. Lake Mary, FL: Charisma House.

Simons, H. and Thompson, J. (2009) *Affective Deprivation Disorder: Does it Constitute a Relational Disorder?* Affectivedeprivation.blogspot.com pp.1–12.

Stanford, A. (2003) *Asperger Syndrome and Long-term Relationships*. London: Jessica Kingsley Publishers.

The NIV Study Bible (1985) Grand Rapids, MI: The Zondervan Corporation (first published in 1973).

Verity, J. (2005) *Positive Approach to Difficult Behaviour*. Victoria: Dementia Care Australia (unpublished workshop paper).

Further reading for couples

Aston, M. (2001) *The Other Half of Asperger Syndrome*. London: The National Autistic Society.

Aston, M. (2003) *Aspergers in Love* London: Jessica Kingsley Publishers.

Chapman, G. (2004) *The Five Love Languages*. Chicago, IL: Northfield Publishing.

Chapman, G. (2007) *The Heart of Five Love Languages*. Chicago, IL: Northfield Publishing.

Henault, I. (2005) *Asperger's Syndrome and Sexuality: From Adolescence Through Adulthood*. London: Jessica Kingsley Publishers.

Jacobs, B. (2006) *Loving Mr. Spock: Understanding an Aloof Lover – Could it be Asperger's Syndrome?* London: Jessica Kingsley Publishers.

Thompson, J. (2009) *Emotionally Dumb: An Overview of Alexithymia*. Australia: Soul Books.

Further reading for women with AS

Attwood, T. and Grandin, T. (2006) *Asperger's and Girls*. Arlington, TX: Future Horizons.

Ernsperger, L., Wendel, D. and Willey, L.H. (2007) *Girls Under the Umbrella of Autism Spectrum Disorders: Practical Solutions for Addressing Everyday Challenges*. Shawnee Mission, KA: Autism Asperger Publishing Company.

Nichols, S., Moravcik, G. and Tetenbaum, S. (2008) *Girls Growing Up on the Autism Spectrum: What Parents and Professionals Should Know About the Pre-teen and Teenage Years*. London: Jessica Kingsley Publishers.

Willey, L.H. (1999) *Pretending to be Normal: Living with Asperger's Syndrome*. London: Jessica Kingsley Publishers.

Further reading for teenagers

Jackson, L. (2002) *Freaks, Geeks and Asperger Syndrome*. London: Jessica Kingsley Publishers.

McCabe, P., McCabe, E. and McCabe, J. (2003) *Living and Loving with Asperger Syndrome*. London: Jessica Kingsley Publishers.

General further reading

Ashfield, J. (2009) *Taking Care of Yourself and Your Family: A Resource Book for Good Mental Health*. Camberwell: Peacock Publications. (Updated edition.)

Kirshenbaum, M. (2003) *The Emotional Energy Factor: The Secrets High-energy People Use to Beat Emotional Fatigue*. New York: Bantum Dell, a division of Random House.

Further reading for parents

Attwood, T. (1998) *Asperger's Syndrome: A Guide for Parents and Professionals*. London: Jessica Kingsley Publishers.

The author does not necessarily endorse everything that is said by other authors referred to in this book.

Internet sites

Research Studies and academic papers: www.tonyattwood.com.au

Grief and loss: www.changingminds.org/disciplines/change_management/ kubler_ross/kubler_ross.htm

AS Support and information: www.aspergersyndrome.org

Strategies on caretaking and codependency: www.livestrong.com/article/ 14672-eliminating-caretaker-behavior/

AfDD: www.maxineaston.co.uk/

ASD Specialist Clinic: www.mindsandhearts.net

The internet sites listed above are not necessarily an endorsement by the author.

To contact the author

www.louiseweston.com.au

Index